Sadie —

It's been too long, but every time I hear "Lady in Red" on the radio I'm right back on that island with you!

Kris Bg

—Stephanie

THE
FISHERMAN'S
WIFE

**SUSTAINABLE RECIPES
AND SALTY STORIES**
STEPHANIE VILLANI AND KEVIN BAY

CONTENTS

CHAPTER 5
BASIC TECHNIQUES
AND HOW-TO'S 186

STORIES OF
THE FISHING LIFE

INTRODUCTION

When Alex and I first started selling fish in the New York City Greenmarkets in 1990, I was amazed at the steady stream of questions I was getting about our life in commercial fishing. Fishermen are known for living an unconventional, anachronistic lifestyle, dependent on the sea, one that many people seem to fantasize about living. Sure, customers ask all the usual questions —like how to keep clams, or how to clean a fish, or how to cook cod— but they also crave something else: a story.

Here they are: the recipes and the stories. This is the story of a fishing family, of piles of ice and smelly, worn fish clothes, of salty water and the mucky, prehistoric smell of low tide. Of mending torn fishing nets and hauling boxes of stiff, bright-eyed fish. Of brining and filleting and packing fish into coolers and making sure every single thing has enough ice. Of building fires and smoking fish in a smoker built out of an old refrigerator. Of driving a truck to the city in the dark and unloading at dawn, setting up our tents and fish boxes and eight hundred pounds of ice, and of talking, talking, talking to folks about fish, telling them how it was caught, answering How do I keep it? How do I cook it? Will it be fresh enough on Monday?

At our house we listen to weather reports constantly. We talk about wind direction and speed, the chance of rain or snow, what the temperature will be when we leave the house at three a.m., and if it will warm up during the day. We work in weather of all kinds with no chance of taking a day off, because this is what we do and people are depending on us. We freeze our fingers and toes off in winter, and wipe the sweat that runs into our eyes in summer, all while unloading seventy-five pound totes of ice. All of our helpers at the market endure working outdoors in all seasons; we teach them tricks to make it through the bitter cold or those hot, humid dog days of summer.

Alex and I live out a basic human transaction: bringing food to the market to be sold. Getting the fish from the boat to the dock is just the beginning. It's a long road from there to the customer's kitchen. None of this process is easy —not on the physical body, not on the psyche, and not financially. That's why Alex named his boat the *Blue Moon*, as a nod to the fact that he earned money as a fisherman once in a blue moon.

Alex grew up in the Chelsea neighborhood of New York City. In 1972, he followed his father out to Copiague, Long Island, for a summer, bought a little clam boat for three hundred dollars and never looked back. He clammed the Great South Bay during the boom in the early 70s, worked offshore lobstering setting sixty traps at a pop, and worked two and three week tuna long-lining trips where the boat was so far offshore they were out of radio contact with land. He learned to run the big boats from a guy called Captain Hate, a notorious Captain Ahab-like tyrant who yelled and screamed at the new recruits, "I've seen more salt water up the crack of my ass than you've seen in a lifetime!" Captain Hate hurled things at the crew and forced them to work nonstop for days (that's where Alex learned to nap anytime, anyplace), but he also taught them by example how to be a successful fisherman.

In the early 90s, Alex moved over to Mattituck on the North Fork of Long Island, a more rural and unspoiled area of farms and rocky beaches, a world away from the Hamptons. He came to go clamming in Long Island Sound right off of Mattituck Inlet. Some smart fisherman had discovered that there was a giant set of surf clams, big five- to six-inch clams with sweet orange meat and a purple inner shell, nestled near the inlet just waiting to be harvested. Dozens of men worked on forty-foot boats blowing the clams off the bottom with pumps, and then catching them with dredges. A tractor trailer loaded full of clams pulled out from the dock every day, most of them bought by Campbell's Soup Company for their clam chowder.

So he could be nearer the surf clam work, Alex rented a small abandoned cottage high on a hill overlooking Mattituck Inlet. It was a little concrete cottage from the 40s, with broken windows and a closet with a dirt floor in the tiny bedroom. It was owned by a wealthy businessman from Staten Island who kept his yacht nearby, and he agreed to rent to Alex for four hundred dollars a month as long as he wasn't bothered for repairs or anything else. Alex installed a hot water heater, hammered in some drywall and tacked down some old carpet scraps that a friend gave him. He also installed an ancient kerosene heater, which he would use as his primary heat source, since the cottage's old electric heater was unreliable and expensive.

Around this time Alex's sister Diane, who lived in Little Italy in Manhattan, suggested he might want to check out the small Greenmarkets in the city. She thought it might be a good way for him to make a little extra money on the side. Many years later she confessed, "I was worried that I might have to support him someday."

So one Saturday in 1988, Alex showed up at the Tribeca Greenmarket in a small pickup truck with a couple of coolers of fish fillets, a few whole fish, and a bag of clams. After two years business got to be so good that he started selling at a new market, Grand Army Plaza in Brooklyn. And that's where we met.

Those early days were fun but also hard work. I remember seeing Alex standing on top of his old grey van, tying totes to the top of it with old trawl line from his lobster pots. His van was so stuffed with coolers and tents and scales that he had no room for the fish totes, big plastic boxes that were the foundation of the fish stand. Every week he would climb up on top of his van and tie twenty-five to thirty of them to the roof, and then drive back home a hundred miles to Mattituck.

I had taken on a second job at the Grand Army Plaza market in 1990 working for an apple and vegetable farmer from the Hudson Valley. All of the farmers and market workers were good friends. We worked through ninety-degree days, snowstorms,

parades, and protests. Occasionally we would go out together after work before the farmers had to climb back in their trucks and drive home.

After a few years my apple farmer boss decided to quit the family farm and go into another line of work. I moved next door and traded selling apples for selling fish.

One night Alex and I were out for dinner and I realized halfway through the evening that we were on a date. We worked together and we enjoyed being together and we always had fun. As time went by the markets got better and better. People were becoming genuinely excited about our fish. I began to spend a lot of weekends out on the North Fork and begrudgingly left Mattituck each week for my job in the city. Alex used to drive me to the train station at five a.m. on Monday mornings. I hated leaving.

Like Alex, I took the leap and chucked the city, my job and my apartment, and left for the North Fork. I told my boss that I was quitting and moving to Mattituck.

"Oh, I was afraid that that might happen," he said, and looked out the window with faraway eyes, "It's a really nice place."

Soon we decided to add a weekday market at Union Square, one that I would do on my own. Alex fished more hours for it, and I drove the truck into New York and sold fish with two other gals. Our two Saturday markets continued to flourish. We put our heads together, worked hard and still managed to have a good time. The business responded by growing bigger and better.

I was able to take over a lot of the paperwork for the business so Alex could spend more time fishing. Luckily I didn't mind dealing with the accountant, the taxes, the fishing reports, the Greenmarket application, the food processing permits, the inspectors, and all the administrative work that has to be done for a business. I even became good at it.

These days we have a young daughter, who shows up occasionally at the markets and loves to cook. When we take our customary winter break over January and February (the worst time to catch fish and the worst time to stand outside selling fish), we take her out of school and go down to the Florida Keys. She goes to the local school where she knows most of the kids by now, and we still have plenty of family time for the beach, miniature golf, sailboat rides, and trips to Key West. It's good to recharge the batteries for another year of working at the markets.

Many of our farmer friends that we met during those early days are still doing the markets, and we have remained close friends. As some of the original farmers have retired, new bakers, farmers, and dairies have stepped in to take their places. Despite the program's stringent regulations, folks are clamoring to get into the GrowNYC Greenmarkets; not only fruit and vegetable farmers and fishermen, but bakers, dairies, flower growers, wineries, cheesemakers, and farmers who raise pigs, sheep, chickens, turkeys, cows, and even emus. It takes a certain kind of hard worker who isn't afraid to try something new and put in many, many hours in addition to their work at home. In return, the Greenmarkets have been embraced by city chefs, restaurants, and the public, and have grown to over fifty markets with over two hundred and thirty producers.

The GrowNYC Greenmarkets have been good to us, allowing us to sell directly to the public. By cutting out the middleman, the fisherman gets to set the price and make more money, and the customer pays a reasonable price for a much fresher product. The added benefit is that the customer can talk directly to us and ask any questions they want about the fish: how to keep it, how it's harvested, and how to cook it. We've been at the markets since 1988, and we have the reputation of a rock solid market stand that has been around a while.

During the season we do not miss any market days (except for reasons that are out of our control, like 9/11 or Hurricane Sandy, both of which shut us down for a few days).

What else is Blue Moon known for?

For a hard-working husband and wife team who take the time to educate customers and answer their every question.

For having reliably fresh fish. We bring in a completely local Long Island catch which changes with the seasons, by the month or even by the week. This includes fish that most folks are familiar with, like flounder and cod, and relatively unknown abundant local fish, like blackfish, blowfish, spearing, or sand shark.

For having excellent customer service, with knowledgeable fishmongers who can help customers choose fish, answer questions, and tell folks how to store it and cook it.

Blue Moon has cultivated a team of experienced and wacky fishmongers that make our stand unique. We have hired artists, activists, former scientists and psychiatrists,

poets, jazz and rock musicians, and corporate refugees whose real hearts are aligned with foodies and farmers. We've had straight, gay, and transgendered folks work for us, and all colors and races too.

Customers can buy their fish and talk about current political actions or protests, a new Broadway show, the upcoming election, or get tips on what event is going on at the Greenmarket this week or the great new restaurant that has been buying our sea bass. We've created a small town feel in the heart of New York City and revel in the transactions between our loyal, repeat customers and our superstar fishmongers. We work hard and still enjoy a great amount of fun and laughter while doing our job.

Stephanie Villani, December 2016

ROUND WHITE FISH

BLACKFISH

Blackfish is a true local fish, native to the Northeast Atlantic and not well-known by most shoppers. Blackfish is also called tautog, the Native American name, and is not to be confused with black sea bass (another local, black-skinned fish).

We refer to it as local grouper or snapper. These fish are found in rocky areas, so our local commercial fishermen use pots or traps to catch them. They are also valued as a recreational catch caught with lines or spearfished.

Blackfish have unusual teeth that look like a toddler's teeth. They use them to crack open oyster or clam shells. We had a small one in our salt water fish tank and used to drop clams in the tank and watch the blackfish crack the shells and eat the meat. They have a white, very firm flesh that tastes sweet, with a line of pin bones down the center of the fillet. They have a very tough skin that is hard to remove; for that reason they are not usually sold whole.

Since the flesh of the blackfish is very firm, you can cook it using any method. It is firm enough to stand up to grilling, poaching, or a chowder or stew.

GRILLED BLACKFISH WITH TARRAGON

Serves 4

1 ¼ to 1 ½ pounds blackfish fillet

2 tablespoons chopped fresh tarragon

2 tablespoons soy sauce

2 tablespoons melted butter

1 tablespoon lemon juice

Combine the tarragon, soy, butter, and lemon juice in a bowl or flat Tupperware container. Add the blackfish fillets and marinate for 45 minutes to one hour under refrigeration.

Grill about 4 minutes per side.

GRILLED BLACKFISH WITH GINGER, LIME AND GARLIC

Serves 2

1 ¼ to 1 ½ pounds blackfish fillet

2 tablespoons soy sauce

1 tablespoon lime juice

2 teaspoons chopped garlic

2 teaspoons chopped ginger

Combine the soy, lime, garlic, and ginger in a bowl or flat Tupperware container. Add the blackfish fillets and marinate for 45 minutes to one hour under refrigeration.

Grill about 4 minutes per side.

POACHED BLACKFISH WITH MUSHROOMS AND VERMOUTH

Serves 4

1 ½ to 1 ¾ pounds blackfish fillet, trimmed of bones and cut into 4 pieces

3 tablespoons olive oil

¼ to ⅓ pound portobello mushrooms, cleaned and thinly sliced

2 teaspoons chopped fresh parsley

1 teaspoon dried tarragon

Salt and pepper to taste

1 tablespoon flour

¾ cup dry white vermouth

Recipe by Harry Smith

Use a pan with a cover large enough to poach the fish. Add 2 tablespoons of olive oil and turn heat to medium-low. Sauté the mushrooms in the covered pan for about 4 minutes. Stir and sauté for another 4 minutes. Remove mushrooms to a bowl and set aside.

Season one side of the blackfish fillets with the parsley, tarragon, salt and pepper. Sprinkle lightly with flour.

Add remaining 1 tablespoon of olive oil to the pan and brown the fillets for about 1 minute. Turn fillet and season the other side with the herbs and the salt and pepper. Sprinkle lightly with flour. Brown for another minute.

Pour mushroom slices and any pan drippings over fillets. Add the vermouth.

Cover the pan and turn heat to medium-high. Cook for about 4 minutes until sauce thickens.

Turn fillets, cover the pan, and let cook another 4 minutes. Serve with mushrooms and sauce spooned over the fish.

BLACK SEA BASS

Sea bass ranges along the entire East Coast, from Maine to Florida. Our local sea bass is so good that I have spent years trying to sell it to customers instead of the Chilean sea bass they ask for (which is horribly overfished). Sea bass caught in the Mediterranean is yet a different fish than North Atlantic or Chilean sea bass.

Black sea bass is one of the more desirable fish —both fishermen and customers treasure its light, delicate taste. We sell small fillets or whole fish. Whole sea bass range from one to about two and a half pounds.

Some facts about sea bass:

- They are hermaphrodites; that is, they are born female and they change sex to become male.

- They are on a very confusing quarterly quota system in New York State; when the quarterly quota is met the stocks are closed until the next quarter begins. I have spent a lot of time explaining this to customers to account for why we have sea bass regularly for a while and then not again for some weeks.

- More sea bass are caught recreationally than commercially (according to the Atlantic Coastal Cooperative Statistics Program), with recreational fishermen using hooks and line, and commercial fishermen using fish pots and trawls.

Sea bass stocks have been under a rebuilding program for several years here in the Northeast. According to the latest report from NOAA in 2012, the stocks are now rebuilt and are not being overfished.

OVEN-BAKED SEA BASS WITH RAMP PESTO

Serves 4

For the Ramp Pesto:

2 tablespoons pine nuts, toasted

2 cups ramp leaves, washed and trimmed of white parts

⅓ cup grated parmesan cheese

1 tablespoon lemon juice

1 teaspoon salt

½ cup olive oil

For the Fish:

1 ½ pounds sea bass fillet, trimmed and pin bones removed

1 ¼ cup panko

½ teaspoon cumin

½ teaspoon salt

2 eggs, beaten

1 tablespoon olive oil or cooking spray

This recipe works with any firm white fish such as fluke or blackfish. Kids especially like fish prepared this way. Since ramps are only available for a short time at the market, use basil, parsley, or scallions when you can't get them. Since ramps have a garlicky flavor I don't use garlic in this recipe. Feel free to do so if you like. You may elect to blanch the ramps before processing them but it's not necessary.

For the Ramp Pesto: To toast pine nuts, place nuts in a small dry pan on medium-low heat. Cook about 3 minutes, shaking the pan every 30 seconds and making sure they do not burn. When they become fragrant take them off the heat.

Roughly chop the ramp leaves and put them in a food processor. Add the pine nuts, parmesan cheese, lemon juice, and salt. Turn the processor on and slowly add the olive oil, pouring in a thin stream.

Taste and add more salt if desired.

For the Fish: Preheat oven to 450 degrees.

Trim the sea bass fillets, cutting out the thin strip of bones that run through the center of the fillet. This will leave you with several small rectangular fillets.

Mix the panko, cumin, and salt together in a shallow bowl. Beat the eggs in another shallow bowl.

Drizzle a large baking sheet with olive oil or use cooking spray.

Dip each fillet in the egg and then in the panko mixture. Place on baking sheet.

Bake for 5 to 6 minutes. Turn each fillet over and bake for another 2 minutes.

Serve fish with ramp pesto or another type of dipping sauce (soy and ginger, mayonnaise-based, or regular pesto).

BROILED SEA BASS WITH OREGANO

Serves 2

1 pound sea bass fillet, pin bones removed

1 tablespoon sesame oil

Salt and pepper to taste

1 tablespoon vegetable oil or cooking spray

2 tablespoons butter

1 teaspoon chopped fresh oregano

Set broiler to high (see note). Put sea bass in a bowl; rub with the sesame oil and season with salt and pepper. Marinate under refrigeration for 15 to 20 minutes.

Oil the bottom of a casserole or baking sheet with the vegetable oil or use cooking spray. Arrange the fish in the casserole, skin side down.

Cut the butter into pieces and distribute evenly over the fish. Sprinkle the fish with the chopped oregano.

Broil for 4 minutes. Baste the fish with the melted butter and return to oven for another 4 minutes. Baste again and check to see if fillets are cooked through.

Serve with the remaining melted butter spooned over the fish.

Note: Broiling guide: Set your pan the proper distance from the heat source depending on the thickness of the fish: 2 inches from heat source for pieces up to ¼ inch thick; 3 inches for pieces up to ¾ inch thick; 4 inches for pieces up to 1 ½ inches thick, 6 inches for thicker pieces.

SEA BASS WITH JAPANESE FLAVORS

Serves 2

2 sea bass fillets (about 7 ounces per fillet), pin bones removed

Salt and pepper to taste

1 tablespoon olive oil or other vegetable oil

½ to 1 pound greens, such as turnip greens, kale, or mizuna

Sea salt to taste

1 tablespoon butter

2 tablespoons concentrated dashi (Japanese fish stock, see note)

½ teaspoon shoyu (soy sauce)

½ teaspoon freshly squeezed lemon juice

Recipe by Chef Hiroko Shimbo, Chef/Instructor, Cookbook Author, and Industry Consultant

Hiroko says, "I live on locally caught, very fresh fish harvested by hard-working Alex, the owner of Blue Moon Fish. His seasonally changing fish is a lifeline in my diet. I am very lucky that I have access to their fish weekly at the Union Square Greenmarket in New York City.

I buy a whole fish, scale it and fillet it in order to ensure the maximum quality of the fish. To those who do not have time to do so, Blue Moon Fish has plenty of filleted fish.

I use this method for a very fresh fish—no teriyaki sauce nor curing in miso sauce. These preparations make the fish taste too sweet and may destroy the natural flavor of very fresh fish. Here is what I often do: use dashi stock (Japanese stock made with kelp and skipjack tuna flakes), shoyu (soy sauce), butter and freshly squeezed lemon juice."

Place a wire rack on a plate or cookie sheet-like pan. Lightly salt the fish fillets on both sides and let them stand for 15 to 20 minutes. During this time the fish exudes surface water which may have some off-flavor. Gently rinse the fish under cold tap water to remove the salt.

Pat dry the fish with paper towels. Salt and pepper the fish.

Heat a skillet over medium heat. Add the olive oil and cook the fish about 3 minutes. Turn over the fish with a spatula. Reduce the heat to low, and cook the fish about 4 minutes.

Divide and transfer the cooked fish onto two dinner plates.

Reheat the skillet over low heat and add the greens with a small pinch of salt. Toss and turn the greens until they are lightly wilted. Divide the greens onto the two plates.

Reheat the skillet over medium-low heat. Add the butter and cook until lightly browned. Add the dashi and cook until it is emulsified. Add the shoyu and lemon juice and cook until the sauce sizzles. Divide the sauce into two plates. Serve the dish while hot.

Note: To make concentrated dashi stock, place 2 cups of water and ¼ ounce kelp in a small pot. Bring to a simmer and cook over low heat for 20 minutes. Remove the kelp from the pot and discard.

Turn the heat to medium-low and add 1 cup katsuobushi fish flakes. Submerge the fish flakes with a spatula and cook 3 minutes. Do not boil. Turn off the heat and let stand 5 minutes. Drain the stock, discarding the fish flakes. Use the leftover dashi stock for miso soup. You may dilute it.

When you are not making dashi in your kitchen you can find an instant, powdered form of dashi. Choose one which does not contain any chemical additives like monosodium glutamate or preservatives.

SEA BASS AREPAS WITH CUMIN, LIME AND CHILE

Serves 2

For the Arepas:

Makes about 8 good-sized arepas

2 cups of arepa flour (two good brands are Harina PAN from Empresas Polar, or Masarepa flour from Goya, see note)

2 teaspoons kosher salt

2 ½ cups warm water

2 tablespoons vegetable oil

For the Fish:

4 fillets sea bass (about 1 pound total), pin bones removed

1 lime, juiced

1 ½ tablespoon minced serrano chile

½ teaspoon sea salt

¼ teaspoon black cumin (or brown cumin)

Paprika to taste

2 tablespoons chopped fresh cilantro

Hot sauce to taste (optional)

1 can black beans (optional)

Arepas are a type of corn cake stuffed with fillings like cheese, fish, pork, black beans, or shrimp. Serve the fish as is if you don't want to make the arepas.

For the Arepas:

Whisk together the arepa flour and salt in a medium sized bowl. Make a well in the center, then add the 2 ½ cups warm water while stirring with a wooden spoon. Keep stirring until all of the dry ingredients are incorporated and no lumps remain. Let the dough rest and hydrate for 5 minutes.

Take a handful of the dough and roll it into a palm-sized ball. Use your other hand to pat the ball down, rotating it and patting until the ball becomes a disk that's about a half inch thick.

Heat 1 tablespoon vegetable oil in a large non-stick skillet over medium heat; add 4 arepas. Cover and cook for 6 to 8 minutes. Flip the arepas and continue cooking uncovered for another 6 to 8 minutes or until golden brown. Transfer to a plate and keep in a warm oven.

Repeat with the remaining tablespoon of vegetable oil and dough.

For the Fish:

Put the fillets in a shallow dish and cover them with the lime juice.

Combine 1 tablespoon of the serrano chile with the sea salt and cumin. Rub one teaspoon of the spice mixture evenly over each fillet.

Oil a cast iron skillet and start your broiler or heat the cast iron on the stove top.

If broiling, cook the fillets skin side up for 8 minutes or until the skin is crispy (see note on page 25). If cooking on the stovetop, start with the fillets skin side down over medium-high heat for 5 minutes, then turn the fillets and continue cooking over medium heat for another 3 to 5 minutes.

Top the fish with the remaining spice mixture and the serrano chiles. Sprinkle with paprika and garnish with cilantro. Add hot sauce if desired.

Plate the fish if not making arepas, or make a pocket in each arepa by splitting them open with a knife, then fill them with the sea bass, spices and black beans.

Note: Arepa flour is a precooked corn flour and should not be confused with masa harina. Arepa flour is sold as masarepa, harina precocida, or masa al instante. It can be found in Latin American groceries.

BLOWFISH

Blowfish, also called puffers or sea squab, are a real Long Island treat. Caught in our local bays, these are the small fish that puff up into a ball when threatened. Traditionally the small tail pieces are deep fried and eaten off the bone like a tiny chicken drumstick. I have heard countless customers recount fishing on the bay as a child and catching tons and tons of blowfish, keeping what they needed for dinner and batting the unwanted puffers back into the water.

I have had questions from customers about whether these fish are poisonous, as the Japanese blowfish (fugu) are. They are not. While Florida blowfish have been known to contain toxins, the blowfish that are found from Chesapeake Bay to New England are safe to eat (as per the FDA website).

Blowfish tails can be found on Long Island menus deep fried and served with tartar sauce. They can also be sautéed, grilled or broiled.

BROILED BLOWFISH TAILS WITH WINE AND SCALLIONS

Serves 2

1 pound blowfish tails, rinsed and patted dry

2 teaspoons olive oil

2 garlic cloves, crushed

1 bunch scallions, sliced lengthwise and then in half, both white and green parts

1 teaspoon cumin

Salt and pepper to taste

½ cup white wine

Set broiler to high (see note on page 25). Coat a large casserole dish with one teaspoon of the olive oil.

In a medium pan over medium-low heat, heat the remaining olive oil. Sauté the garlic and scallions over medium-low heat until soft, about 4 to 5 minutes.

Arrange the blowfish tails in the casserole dish in one layer (they should not touch each other) and season with the cumin, salt and pepper.

Pour the wine over the fish and add the garlic and scallions on top.

Broil for 8 to 10 minutes until fish is browned. Check the largest blowfish tail with a thin-bladed knife to see if it is cooked through.

Serve with the pan juices spooned on top of the fish.

BUTTERFISH

Butterfish are small, blue-skinned fish that only weigh a few ounces each. While I wouldn't exactly call them a trash fish, they are usually very cheap and not familiar to most shoppers. They are plentiful at certain times of the year, but during the summer they usually move out into the deep ocean, so only a handful are available during that time.

Butters are mild and white-fleshed; you will need two or three per person. For a long time I thought butterfish had no scales whatsoever; they do, but they are so small that you can just rinse them off with water and pat dry.

I recently discovered that the term "butterfish" has been co-opted by west coast fishmongers to rename another fish called escolar, which is delicious, oily, and causes severe gastrointestinal issues. Do not be fooled by this re-naming campaign! Our Atlantic butterfish are always sold whole, not filleted.

Butters can be roasted in the oven, grilled, steamed, or pan-fried. They are among the easiest of whole fish to cook, and they are a good choice if you have never cleaned a fish before. It's easiest to cut off the head and remove the stomach in one swipe, but you can leave the heads on if you like.

PAN-FRIED BUTTERFISH

Serves 2

1 pound butterfish (about 4 fish, headed and gutted)

⅔ cup cornmeal

⅔ cup all-purpose flour

Salt and pepper to taste

2 tablespoons butter

2 tablespoons olive oil

Lemon, chopped fresh herbs, or any sauce for garnish

Clean the butterfish by cutting the head off on a diagonal, making sure you cut out the stomach cavity. Rinse under running water and pat dry.

Put cornmeal and flour in a shallow bowl. Season with salt and pepper and mix well.

In a skillet large enough to contain the fish, melt the butter and the olive oil over medium-high heat.

Dredge the fish in the cornmeal/flour mixture, coating on both sides and shaking off the excess.

Fry the fish until cooked through, about 3 to 4 minutes on each side, depending on the size of the fish.

Check the fish with a thin-bladed knife down to the bone to see if it is cooked.

Serve with a squeeze of lemon, a handful of chopped herbs, or any sauce you like.

CORNMEAL CRUSTED BUTTERFISH FILLETS WITH SPICY CHARRED HEIRLOOM TOMATO SAUCE

Serves 2

For Fish:

4 butterfish (1 to 1 ½ pounds total)

2 cups fine semolina

1 cup all-purpose flour

1 to 2 tablespoons Old Bay seasoning

1 to 1 ½ cups buttermilk

Salt to taste

Spicy Charred Heirloom Tomato Sauce

4 to 6 large ripe heirloom tomatoes (use beefsteak tomatoes if you can't get heirlooms), quartered

2 to 4 jalapeño peppers

8 to 10 Thai chilies

10 garlic cloves

4 to 6 large shallots

2 to 4 tablespoons fish sauce

2 to 4 tablespoons lime juice

1 to 2 tablespoons sugar depending on how ripe the tomatoes are

10 sprigs of cilantro, chopped

Recipe by Chef Soulayphet Schwader, Khe-Yo, New York City

For the Fish:

Mix all dry ingredients together.

Fillet butterfish, leaving skin on. Soak fillets in buttermilk for 10 minutes.

Toss fillets in flour mixture and lightly fry in oil at 375 degrees until golden brown (about 2 to 3 minutes per side). Season lightly with salt.

For the Spicy Charred Heirloom Tomato Sauce:

Char all the tomatoes, jalapeño, chilies, garlic and shallots over an open flame or on a hot grill until black (about 5 to 8 minutes). Set tomatoes aside. Wrap the jalapeño, chilies, garlic and shallots in foil and roast in a 375 degree oven for 10 to 15 minutes until slightly soft.

In a mortar and pestle, take the roasted jalapeño, chilies, garlic and shallots and grind to a chunky mixture. Add the tomatoes and season with fish sauce and lime juice. Check flavor looking for sweet, sour and spicy. If the tomatoes are not naturally sweet adjust with sugar.

Pour sauce over the fried butterfish; sprinkle with chopped cilantro and serve.

COD

Culturally and historically, cod is the most important fish in the North Atlantic region. It has been caught and traded since the time of the Vikings; whole economies of towns and cities have been built on catching cod. The Massachusetts House of Representatives to this day displays a wooden carving of a codfish, representing the importance of the fish to the community.

In the early 1990s, the Northwestern Atlantic cod fishery collapsed. Regulations were put in place to rebuild the stocks, which have rebounded, but are nowhere near the amounts seen in the past. Right now the Pacific and Northeast Atlantic stocks are doing fairly well, but our local Northwestern Atlantic stocks have a way to go to recover.

We sell cod at the fish stand when it is in season (October to March), and we do not have large amounts available. In the last few years we have seen an increase in the amount and the size of the fish landed, which is good news.

Codfish is known for having parasites; at the fillet house the cod fillets are laid out on a light board and any worms removed with tweezers. The worms are not really harmful if eaten cooked, but are unappetizing to say the least! It follows that this fish should not be eaten raw; the soft, flaky flesh is too soft for sashimi anyway.

BEER BATTERED COD

Serves 6

2 pounds cod fillet, cut into 4-inch pieces, center pin bones removed

2 quarts cooking oil (we use canola)

2 cups all-purpose flour

18 ounces beer (1 ½ bottles; we use Heineken or Anchor Steam)

3 teaspoons hot paprika

3 teaspoons kosher salt

2 teaspoons black pepper

2 teaspoons garlic powder

In a large, deep pot, heat oil over medium-high. The oil is hot enough when a pinch of flour dropped in it sizzles.

Mix flour, beer, paprika, salt, pepper and garlic powder together in a large bowl to make a batter.

Dip cod pieces in batter and fry in hot oil, about 4 minutes per piece, until golden brown.

Serve with malt vinegar or tartar sauce.

BAKED COD WITH HONEY MUSTARD AND HERB CRUST

Serves 2

¾ to 1 pound cod or other thick fillet, cut in two pieces

2 tablespoons honey

2 tablespoons Dijon mustard

½ cup panko

2 tablespoons olive oil

2 teaspoons chopped fresh thyme

2 teaspoons chopped fresh parsley

These recipes for baked cod with a crust can be used on a variety of thick fish fillets, including a few kinds that we don't sell: sea bass, blackfish, salmon, tilefish, striped bass, sea trout, bluefish or fluke.

Set the oven to 425 degrees. Cover a baking sheet with foil and set the cod fillets on it.

In a small bowl mix the honey and mustard together. Spoon it over the fish, taking care to cover the top and sides well.

In another bowl mix the panko, olive oil, and herbs together. Using your fingers, press the panko mixture on top of the honey and mustard covered fish.

Bake about 10 to 15 minutes depending on the thickness of the fish. (10 minutes per inch is the general rule.)

BAKED COD WITH HORSERADISH CRUST

Serves 2

¾ to 1 pound cod or other thick fillet, cut in two pieces

½ cup panko

3 tablespoons prepared horseradish, drained

2 tablespoons chopped fresh dill

2 tablespoons sour cream

1 teaspoon salt

Set the oven to 425 degrees. Cover a baking sheet with foil and set the cod fillets on it.

In a small bowl mix the panko, horseradish, dill, sour cream and salt together. Using your fingers, press the panko mixture on top of the fish.

Bake about 10 to 15 minutes depending on the thickness of the fish. (10 minutes per inch is the general rule.)

SALT COD WITH POLENTA

Serves 2 to 4

For the Fish:

One package salt cod, 1 to 2 pounds, soaked for 24 to 48 hours

¼ cup olive oil

One head garlic (about 8 cloves), chopped

Juice of one lemon

One bunch fresh parsley, chopped

For Polenta:

4 cups chicken stock

1 ¾ cup polenta (not instant)

Fresh pepper to taste

This is a traditional Northern Italian dish that Alex's family always ate around Christmastime. Sometimes it was made with a tomato sauce with basil and parsley, but Alex always cooks this version with lots of garlic and parsley, and it is always served with polenta.

Salt cod is cod that has been preserved by salting and drying. When using salt cod, start a day or two ahead and soak the dried cod in a bowl of water set in the refrigerator. Change the water 3 or 4 times a day to remove the salt. (Some cooks soak the cod in milk instead of salt.)

Rinse the salt cod fillets and pat dry. Chop into pieces roughly 4 inches by 2 inches.

Heat olive oil over medium-low heat. Add the garlic and the fresh lemon juice. Cook for 3 to 4 minutes.

Add the fish and turn the heat to medium. Add the parsley and turn the fish to coat.

Cook 4 to 5 minutes until golden brown. Remove to a plate.

Serve on a bed of polenta.

For Polenta:

In a heavy pot bring stock to a high simmer. Add the polenta and stir. Continue to stir every few minutes until mixture thickens, about 15 to 20 minutes.

Add the fresh pepper and stir. When mixture pulls away from side of the pan it is done. Polenta should be soft and creamy, not runny.

DOGFISH/SAND SHARK

The only type of shark that we sell are plentiful on Eastern Long Island and are called dogfish (also called sand shark). They average around 3 to 4 feet long and possess rows of flat, blunt teeth used for grinding crustaceans and mollusks. We had one in our salt water fish tank once; it ate all the other fish in the tank and grew so fast that we had to release it back into the Sound.

Dogfish are considered a trash fish and there isn't much of a market for them in this country; most customers are just not familiar with this fish. There was a recent effort by the National Marine Fisheries Service to encourage fishermen to catch more dogfish. There are tons of dogfish in the Northeast, but most are shipped to the UK to be served as fish and chips.

Dogfish have a very firm, very mild lean flesh, which does well when marinated. It can be cooked by any method because of its firm, dense texture: grilled, poached, fried, broiled or baked.

Since this is a shark with no bone structure, just cartilage, the fish needs to be handled properly and cooked right away to prevent the ammonia-like smell that can develop. Some people soak it in milk or salt water before cooking, but we never do; we just make sure it is properly iced and cooked (or frozen) immediately.

DOGFISH WITH SESAME SEEDS

Serves 2

1 pound dogfish fillet, trimmed of any skin or pieces of cartilage

4 tablespoons mirin

4 tablespoons soy sauce

4 tablespoons lemon juice

2 tablespoons sesame oil

2 tablespoons sesame seeds

¼ cup vegetable oil

Lemon wedges

Cooked rice or noodles (optional)

Slice the fillet crosswise into 1-inch pieces.

Mix together the mirin, soy sauce, lemon juice, sesame oil, and sesame seeds. Place the dogfish pieces in the marinade and refrigerate. Marinate for 30 minutes.

Warm the vegetable oil in a pan over medium-high heat. When hot, put the dogfish pieces in the pan. Pour the marinade over the fish.

Sauté for 2 to 3 minutes, turning once. Remove to a plate lined with paper towels.

Serve the fish with lemon wedges for an appetizer, or over rice or noodles for a main dish.

BAKED DOGFISH WITH TOMATO, RED ONION, AND OLIVES

Serves 2

1 pound dogfish, trimmed of any skin or pieces of cartilage and cut into two pieces

1 teaspoon olive oil

⅓ cup white wine

Salt to taste

⅓ cup sliced red onion

⅓ cup pitted and roughly chopped Kalamata olives

½ cup tomato, seeded and roughly chopped

1 tablespoon chopped fresh chives

1 tablespoon chopped fresh parsley

I have given this recipe out at the fish stand for two decades. You may substitute almost any other type of fish (blackfish, striped bass, fluke, sea bass, sea trout). Use any combination of fresh herbs you can find at the market.

Set oven to 400 degrees. Brush the bottom of a baking sheet or cast iron pan with the olive oil.

Set the fish in the pan; pour the wine over the fish. Season with the salt.

Arrange the onion slices, olives, and tomato over the fish. Sprinkle the chives and parsley on top.

Bake for 15 minutes. Check the fish with a thin-bladed knife and return to the oven if not cooked through (another 2 to 3 minutes).

MONKFISH

The fishermen call this fish "belly," or "anglerfish," or "ocean blowfish." It's a bizarre-looking monster that used to be considered a trash fish. A 2013 stock assessment by NOAA Fisheries found that "monkfish are not overfished and are not subject to overfishing in both northern and southern areas" (of the East Coast). Fishermen are allowed a certain number of days at sea to catch monkfish, which are included in the Northeast multispecies fishery (also called the groundfish fishery).

You may recognize another name for monkfish —poor man's lobster— as the fillet, which is boneless and comes from the tail, is dense and mild and has the texture of lobster meat. Monkfish will eat anything, even each other. Alex says that he has caught monkfish with large lobsters in their bellies.

Since monk is so firm, it is ideal for use in stews and chowders. I have found good results cutting it into pieces and stir frying, or cutting it into medallions and sautéing in a bit of wine. It can also be baked whole or cut up and used as kabobs on the grill.

Monk fillet has a gray membrane surrounding it that should be removed. It has a rather gritty texture, which is not all that pleasant to eat but will not harm you. If you cannot remove it by peeling it away with a sharp knife, it's possible to cook the whole fillet and peel off the membrane after cooking and before serving. Monk also makes a dynamite mild smoked fish, even though it is not fatty at all. I like to cut it into pieces and marinate the smoked fish in olive oil; the oil picks up the smoky flavor of the fish and can be used in cooking.

MONKFISH-VEGETABLE STIR FRY

Serves 2

1 pound monkfish fillet, membrane removed and cut into 1-inch chunks

Salt and pepper to taste

2 tablespoons grapeseed oil

3 cloves garlic, slivered

1-inch piece of ginger, peeled and slivered

½ white onion, sliced (about 1 cup)

1 medium carrot, julienned into 1 to 1 ½ inch pieces

½ cup water

½ pound asparagus (about ½ bunch), washed and cut into 1-inch pieces

3 ounces snow peas, trimmed and cut in half

2 tablespoons soy sauce

1 tablespoon lemon juice

2 teaspoons sesame oil

1 teaspoon hot chili oil

Salt and pepper to taste

Lemon wedges

Cooked rice or noodles (optional)

Put the monkfish chunks on a plate and season with salt and pepper.

Heat the grapeseed oil in a large skillet over high heat. When the oil is hot place the fish in the skillet.

Cook the fish for 2 minutes per side; remove to a plate. Turn the heat to medium-high.

Add the garlic and ginger. Sauté for 1 minute. Add the onion and carrot; sauté for 2 to 3 minutes.

Add ½ cup water to the pan. Add the asparagus and the snow peas. Add the soy sauce, the lemon juice, the sesame oil, and the chili oil. Cook for 3 to 4 minutes.

Turn the heat to high and add the monkfish. Season with salt and pepper and mix the fish with the vegetables.

Heat through for about 2 to 3 minutes. Serve in pasta bowls with plenty of broth and with lemon wedges to squeeze over dish. May be served over noodles or rice or as is.

BLACKENED MONKFISH CAESAR SALAD

Serves 2 to 3 as a Main Dish or 6 as an Appetizer

1 pound of monkfish fillet, membrane removed and cut into ½ inch thick medallions

¾ pound unsalted butter (3 sticks), melted

Seasoning Mix:

1 tablespoon sweet paprika

1 teaspoon salt

1 teaspoon onion powder

1 teaspoon garlic powder

½ teaspoon ground white pepper

½ teaspoon ground black pepper

½ teaspoon dried thyme leaves

½ teaspoon dried oregano leaves

½ to ⅛ teaspoon cayenne pepper (optional)

For the Salad:

12 to 16 ounces salad greens

12 to 16 croutons

3 tablespoons grated parmesan cheese

2 teaspoons Caesar dressing

Blackening fish will create a crispy, spicy crust around the fish while keeping the insides deliciously moist. Be forewarned, this will smoke up your kitchen, but it's worth it!

Any thick fillet is appropriate for this cooking method, including tilefish, sea trout, and blackfish. Make sure that the fillets aren't more than ¾ inch thick, preferably keeping them to ½ inch thickness.

Heat a large cast-iron skillet over high heat for at least 10 minutes. Keep heating past the smoking stage until you start to see an ashy white color develop in the skillet (the skillet can't be too hot for this dish).

Thoroughly combine the seasoning mix ingredients in a small bowl. Using tongs, dip the monkfish medallions in the melted butter so they are completely coated, then dredge them in the seasoning mix, patting the spices on generously with your hands. When they are coated, place as many of them as you can into the hot un-oiled skillet, being careful not to crowd the pan.

Pour half of the remaining melted butter over the fish (caution: the butter may flame up momentarily and there will be smoke). Cook them uncovered over the same high heat until the undersides look charred, about 2 to 3 minutes (the time will vary based on the fish's thickness and the heat of the skillet).

Turn the medallions over and again pour butter on top. Cook another 2 to 3 minutes. Repeat with any remaining medallions.

Toss the salad greens and croutons with the parmesan cheese and the dressing. Plate the salad, then add the blackened monk.

MONKFISH LIVER

Occasionally at the fish stand we have monkfish liver for sale. You will find it made into a pâté in Japanese restaurants; it is rich and delicious with a silky texture. We describe it as the "fois gras of the sea." It can be sautéed or steamed, and sliced for an appetizer. Because it is so rich, it serves best as an appetizer rather than a main dish.

POACHED MONKFISH LIVER

Serves 4 as an Appetizer

¾ to 1 pound monkfish liver
(1 large or 2 small livers)

4 cups water

10 peppercorns

1 bay leaf

5 or 6 parsley sprigs

2 tablespoons salt

3 scallions, chopped, for garnish

For Dipping Sauce:

4 tablespoons soy sauce

½ teaspoon sesame oil

½ teaspoon olive oil

½ teaspoon rice vinegar

½ teaspoon grated ginger

½ teaspoon lemon juice

¼ teaspoon hot sauce

We have been giving this recipe out for years at the fish stand. Wrap the liver in a piece of cheesecloth or plastic wrap and poach it until cooked through; serve with a dipping sauce.

Remove any veins or membrane on the liver with a sharp knife. Rinse and pat dry.

Place liver in a piece of cheesecloth or plastic wrap and roll into a cylinder. Tie off the ends with kitchen twine.

In a large saucepan add the water and the peppercorns, bay leaf, parsley, and salt. Turn heat to medium-low.

Add the liver to the pan and cover. Poach for 45 minutes.

Remove from pan and let cool. Chill in refrigerator for several hours or overnight.

Unwrap and slice into rounds. Serve with chopped scallions and dipping sauce.

For Dipping Sauce:
Whisk all ingredients together in small bowl.

PORGY

This is the trash fish you should be eating right now! Porgy, otherwise known as scup, is over 200% rebuilt as far as the species biomass goes (according to the Atlantic States Marine Fisheries Commission's Fishery Management Plan for the 2015 Scup Fishery). In the last several years, the fishermen have been trying to target areas away from the porgies, as there are too many and they fill their nets to the brim with thousands of pounds of them. If you are looking for a sustainable fish, this is it!

Porgy has a reputation as being bony; for that reason in years past we never sold porgy fillets at the fish stand. Since there are so many around now and the fish Alex lands are larger, we have them filleted and sell both fillets and whole porgy at the market. Our customers buy both. Porgy is known as a pan fish, meaning the small-sized fillet is perfect to pan fry or steam. This is also a great fish to bake whole in a salt crust.

I notice that chefs are experimenting with new names for the same old porgy: "Montauk sea bream" is the latest one. I think that is a sign of a fish going from "trash fish" to a desirable entrée, like skate and monkfish have. At Blue Moon we're still calling it porgy. Whether or not you're on trend with the name, you should give this fish a try.

WHOLE GRILLED PORGY WITH OREGANO AND LEMON

Serves 2

1 whole porgy, 1 ½ to 2 pounds, scaled and gutted

⅓ cup olive oil

3 teaspoons chopped fresh oregano

½ lemon, juiced

1 teaspoon salt

½ teaspoon pepper

8 to 10 sprigs of oregano, about 3 to 4 inches long

2 lemons, washed, halved and cut into half-moons

With a sharp knife, score the porgy on either side, down to the bone, from the head to the tail.

Mix together olive oil, chopped oregano, lemon juice, salt and pepper to make a marinade. Stuff the cuts with the sprigs of oregano and a few pieces of lemon. Stuff the stomach cavity with more oregano and lemon slices.

Put the fish in a shallow bowl or flat Tupperware container and pour the marinade over it. Turn the fish over and make sure it is completely coated by the marinade. Marinate for 45 minutes under refrigeration.

Grill, cooking about 8 to 10 minutes a side. Use a knife to check whether the flesh is cooked through down to the bone.

CAJUN SPICED PORGY FILLETS

Serves 2

1 pound porgy fillets (4 to 5 pieces)

1 cup all-purpose flour

1 teaspoon Cajun spice

¼ cup olive oil

Lemon wedges

Salt to taste

Cut out the thin line of bones that runs down each porgy fillet (if you end up with two small strips of fish, that's fine).

Combine the flour and the Cajun spice on a plate or a shallow dish and mix with a fork. Dip the fillets in the flour mixture and shake off the excess.

Heat the olive oil in a nonstick pan over medium to medium-high heat. When the oil is hot place the fillets in the pan. Cook 2 to 3 minutes per side.

Remove from pan and drain on paper towels. Season with salt and a squeeze of lemon.

SEA ROBIN

Sea robins are true trash fish. Most of the local fishermen, commercial and recreational, consider them a nuisance as they compete with more desirable fish like striped bass or fluke. They are mostly used as bait for fish pots or as chum or fertilizer. We sell them at the fish stand for $1.50 per pound; the cheapest fish we offer.

Sea robins make grunting or barking sounds when caught. They have oversized pectoral fins that look like wings, and small feelers on either side that look like legs, which they use to dig around the ocean bottom to look for food.

The head is so bony that we recommend it be cut off and discarded. The flesh is meaty and white and firm, and holds up well in a soup or a stew. Our European customers recognize sea robin as gurnard, commonly used in bouillabaisse.

"Can you eat sea robin?" is a very common question at the fish stand —of course you can! We have cut the heads off and thrown the tails on the grill, or roasted the tails in the oven. Sea robins have a different bone structure than other round fish, but they can be filleted and cooked as you would any other type of firm, white fish. The fillets are much smaller; they look like fish fingers, about 3 to 4 inches long and ½ to ¾ of an inch thick. Choose the largest sea robin you can if you want to fillet it.

Years ago we sold sea robins (and any other odd-looking sea creatures that came up in the net) to a chef with a very well-regarded East Village restaurant. He filleted the robins and poached the meat in butter. When Alex and I visited the restaurant we tried the dish and it was incredible. Alex said to me, "Don't ever tell anyone that I ordered sea robin and paid 20 bucks for it!"

ROASTED SEA ROBIN TAILS WITH GARLIC, CAPERS, AND DILL

Serves 2

2 sea robin tails, about 1 ½ to 2 pounds total

1 tablespoon olive oil

¾ cup fish stock or chicken stock

Salt and pepper to taste

2 large garlic cloves, slivered

1 tablespoon capers, rinsed

1 tablespoon chopped fresh dill

Since the head of the sea robin is so bony and contains hardly any meat, we usually cut it off and discard it. First cut the line of spines off with kitchen shears, and cut through the bone just behind the head. Scale the tail and remove any viscera from the stomach cavity, and the robin tail is ready to use.

If you want to remove the skin from the tail, cut through the bone just behind the head, leaving the head attached. Take a sharp knife and make a cut just under the skin on either side of the top back of the fish. Grab the head and pull it off; the skin will peel off with it.

Set oven to 400 degrees. Brush a shallow baking dish with the oil and heat in the oven for a few minutes. Add the sea robin tails, cavity up.

Pour the stock over the fish and season with salt and pepper. Scatter the garlic, capers and dill over the fish. Roast uncovered for 20 minutes. Check fish with a thin-bladed knife; if not completely cooked return to oven and check every 3 or 4 minutes until cooked through.

GALLINELLA AL VAPORE (STEAMED SEA ROBIN)

Serves 4

2 sea robins, about 1 ½ pounds each, gutted with gills removed (scaling is not necessary)

2 bunches of scallions, washed and trimmed of the root and white part

Olive oil for drizzling

Salt and pepper to taste

Lemon wedges

Recipe by Ruggero Vanni

Lay the green portion of the scallions on the fish poacher's rack to form an even bed. Put spacers on the bottom of the fish poacher so the rack will sit ½ inch above the bottom of a poacher (four tablespoons turned upside down do the trick). Pour enough water in the poacher for the level to reach ½ inch.

Wash the fish thoroughly inside and out. Place them on top of the scallions on the fish poacher's rack, making sure they don't touch each other. Place the rack in the poacher and close the lid.

Place the poacher on the stovetop (preferably over two burners so the heat is more even). Set the temperature to high. As soon as the water comes to a boil, set the temperature to low to produce a constant gentle steam. Cook until the skin of the fish starts to break along the dorsal fin, about 6 minutes. Remove from the stovetop and let sit for 10 minutes with the lid on.

Remove rack from the poacher and gently slide the fish onto the serving plate. Cut the skin along the dorsal fin and remove the skin from both sides (the scales will make the skin quite rigid and it should pull off easily).

Drizzle some good olive oil over the fish. Season with salt and pepper, and serve with lemon slices.

STRIPED BASS

The comeback of striped bass in the Northeast is a big success story. Back in the 1980s the striped bass population collapsed, and we were on the verge of losing the fishery —one that was once so abundant that they were used to fertilize farm fields. The Atlantic States Marine Fisheries Commission stepped in and implemented a management plan for striped bass from Maine to North Carolina. The stock was rebuilt in 1995, and the 2015 stock assessment found that striped bass are not overfished and not subject to overfishing (NOAA FishWatch).

We are still under some very strict rules for catching striped bass commercially. There are state-by-state catch quotas, minimum and maximum size restrictions, gear restrictions, and seasonal closures to protect spawning populations. For 2016, New York State commercial fishermen were allowed 196 tags for fish to be caught June 1st through December 15th. Each fish must be tagged with special tags issued by the New York State Department of Environmental Conservation that fishermen must buy. Commercial fishermen must possess a special striped bass license as well as a commercial food fish license, and can only keep fish between 28 and 38 inches in length.

Recreational fishing regulations are different, with different seasons and different minimum and maximum sizes for keepers. New York State is a big sport fishing state, and recreational fishermen landed 19 million pounds in 2012 and 24 million pounds of striped bass in 2013, while commercial harvests have averaged 7 million pounds in each of the past several years.

Striped bass fillets are thick, firm and tasty without being oily; the flavor of wild-caught bass is much more delicious than that of farm-raised bass (which is a hybrid and is usually sold whole or in very small fillets). As with all of our local fish, we eat lots of it in season and freeze up a batch to get us partway through the off season.

Since the fish is so thick and firm, you can cook it any way. In the summer and fall we grill it; in the fall and winter we roast it in the oven. It is mild enough and will hold its shape in a chowder or fish stew.

SPICE-RUBBED STRIPED BASS

Serves 2

Cinnamon Spice Rub

2 tablespoons ground red pepper

1 teaspoon ground cinnamon

1 teaspoon ground cumin

1 teaspoon kosher salt

Mix all spices together. Store in a tightly sealed container.

Turmeric Spice Rub

1 teaspoon ground turmeric

1 teaspoon sweet paprika

1 teaspoon ground cumin

1 teaspoon kosher salt

½ teaspoon ground garlic

½ teaspoon black pepper

Mix all spices together. Store in a tightly sealed container.

For the Bass:

1 large fillet striped bass, about 1 pound

We use a dry spice rub on ribs quite often; it is easy and very flavorful. Here are two different rubs that work well on the meaty, firm flesh of the striped bass. It's easy to throw on the grill, or you can use a grill pan on the stovetop or broil in the oven.

Trim the bass of any ragged edges or stray bones and cut it into two or three smaller pieces.

Using one of the above rubs, rub each piece of the fish with a liberal amount of spice, covering the fillet entirely.

Put on a plate and cover with plastic wrap, or use a Tupperware container with a lid. Refrigerate the fish for 3 to 4 hours, letting the spice penetrate the flesh.

Prepare a grill or grill pan. Grill the fillets, 4 to 5 minutes per side, depending on the thickness of the fillet.

STRIPED BASS IN PARCHMENT PAPER

Serves 4

1 ½ to 2 pounds striped bass,
cut into four portions, pin bones
removed

1 bunch scallions (about 12),
washed, roots trimmed

2 small tomatoes,
sliced ¼ inch thick

1 lemon, sliced ¼ inch thick

4 tablespoons butter

Salt and pepper to taste

4 tablespoons white wine

This is a great method to cook nearly any kind of fish fillet, thick or thin, mild or oily. The fish is wrapped in parchment paper and layered with vegetables, spices, and a little bit of liquid to keep the fish moist. Wrap it well and bake in the oven, 5 or 6 minutes for thin fillets like flounder, 10 to 12 minutes for thicker fillets like striped bass. My daughter loves to help me pack and wrap the packages, and it makes a striking presentation for dinner guests when you slit the package and the fragrant steam is released.

Here we use striped bass, which is usually on the thick side. Feel free to improvise with whatever ingredients you have on hand.

Preheat oven to 400 degrees.

Cut a piece of parchment paper about 18 inches long. Place four scallion tops in the middle of the sheet.

Lay one of the bass fillets on top of the scallions. Put 2 tomato slices and 2 lemon slices on top of the bass.

Measure one tablespoon of butter and break into pieces. Lay the butter pieces on top of the fish. Season with salt and pepper to taste.

Fold the top and bottom edges of the parchment over about an inch or two. Just before you get ready to close the package, drizzle one tablespoon of wine over the fish. Carefully bring the left and right sides of the parchment paper together, and fold together to form a seam.

Fold over the top and bottom edges once or twice to seal the seam. You should have a tightly wrapped package of fish. Prepare three more packages like the first one and put on a baking sheet.

Bake about 8 to 10 minutes. Serve one package per person, slitting the parchment and taking care not to burn yourself with the steam.

STRIPED BASS WITH PAPRIKA BUTTER

Serves 4

1 ½ pounds striped bass, cut in 4 pieces

Cooking spray or 1 tablespoon vegetable oil

½ cup butter, melted (one stick)

1 tablespoon lemon juice

1 teaspoon sweet paprika

½ teaspoon salt

¼ cup chopped fresh parsley

Preheat oven to 425 degrees.

Spray baking sheet with cooking spray, or brush with vegetable oil, and lay the fish fillets on it.

Mix butter, lemon juice, paprika, and salt in small bowl. Brush fish with the paprika butter sauce.

Sprinkle fillets with chopped parsley. Bake for 6 minutes; baste with remaining sauce, and bake for another 6 minutes. Check fish with a thin-bladed knife; if not completely cooked return to oven and check every 3 or 4 minutes until cooked through.

SWORDFISH

According to NOAA's FishWatch 2013, the North Atlantic swordfish population is fully rebuilt, at approximately 14 percent above its target level. The 2012 NOAA Fisheries website noted that "Today, North Atlantic swordfish is one of the most sustainable seafood choices" and the rebuilding of this stock is "one of the greatest success stories of U.S. and international fisheries management." They go on to observe that when consumers "buy North Atlantic Swordfish harvested by U.S. vessels, they are supporting one of the most environmentally responsible pelagic longline fisheries in the world."

If only this fact were well known! Sustainability of the swordfish stocks is by far the most asked question about swordfish. The second most asked question is about the likelihood of mercury contamination. This is a valid concern. Sword is a big predator, and methylmercury does accumulate in its flesh. Consequently, you should limit your consumption as per FDA guidelines to 8 ounces per week.

That being said, we catch a lot of swordfish off Long Island in the season (June through October), and the quality of the fish we have been getting the past few years has been phenomenal. It often has a rosy pinkish or orangey color, due to the fish's diet.

Some facts about swordfish:

- Their long, flat bill is used to slash at prey. It is one of the fastest fish around, swimming at speeds reaching 50 mph.

- They are cold-blooded but have a mechanism that allows their eyes and brain to remain heated.

- NOAA operates a Cooperative Tagging Center, which is a volunteer tagging program for billfish (including swordfish), tunas, and other highly migratory species in the Atlantic Ocean. Fish are electronically tagged and data relayed to scientists via satellite.

Swordfish has been known to contain parasites; for that reason we do not recommend that it be eaten raw. Be sure that it is cooked all the way through when you prepare it.

GRILLED SWORDFISH WITH PONZU SAUCE

Serves 4

1 ½ pounds swordfish steaks
(2 or 3 pieces)

3 tablespoons ponzu sauce

1 tablespoon lemon juice

½ teaspoon salt

¼ teaspoon freshly ground
black pepper

Mix ponzu sauce, lemon juice, salt and pepper in a large bowl. Marinate the swordfish steaks in the mixture for 30 to 45 minutes under refrigeration.

Grill, cooking about 4 to 5 minutes on a side until fish is cooked through. Serve with lemon wedges.

ORANGE-LEMON SWORDFISH STEAKS

Serves 4

1 ½ pounds swordfish steaks
(2 or 3 pieces)

3 tablespoons chopped
fresh basil

2 tablespoons olive oil

1 tablespoon butter, softened

2 teaspoons lemon zest

2 teaspoons orange zest

1 teaspoon red pepper flakes

Lemon wedges

Mix basil, olive oil, butter, lemon zest, orange zest, and red pepper flakes in a large bowl. Marinate the swordfish steaks in the mixture for 30 to 45 minutes under refrigeration.

Grill, cooking about 4 to 5 minutes on a side until fish is cooked through. Serve with lemon wedges.

SWORDFISH BARCAIOLA

Serves 4 to 6

For the Barcaiola Sauce:

1 ⅓ cups extra virgin olive oil

3 tablespoons chopped garlic

⅓ cup anchovy fillets, drained

1 cup sliced pepperoncini

1 cup capers, drained

1 cup martini pearl onions (we use Miss Scarlett brand pickled in vermouth)

⅓ cup lemon juice

For the Broccoli Rabe:

2 tablespoons + ¼ cup olive oil

1 large clove garlic, chopped

1 bunch broccoli rabe, trimmed and washed

Pinch of salt

½ cup water

For the Polenta:

4 ½ cups water, separated

1 teaspoon salt

1 cup corn meal

1 cup cream

⅛ pound butter (about 4 tablespoons)

¼ cup Parmigiano Reggiano or Grana Padano

For the Fish:

1 ½ pounds swordfish, cut into 6 pieces

¼ cup olive oil

Recipe by Chef Carmen Quagliata
Union Square Cafe, New York City

Barcaiola means boatman; the barcaiola sauce is made of ingredients that can be kept on the boat without refrigeration and used to dress a fish dinner after a day on the water.

For the Barcaiola Sauce:

In a non-reactive pot, pour in ⅓ cup of the olive oil and heat. Add garlic and anchovies and sauté until anchovies are "dissolved." Add the rest of the ingredients plus the remaining cup of olive oil to pot and simmer very gently for 5 minutes. Purée with hand mixer to a coarse purée. Store in covered container and refrigerate overnight. Remove the next day before using to allow the sauce to warm up to room temperature, about 1 hour.

For the Broccoli Rabe:

Heat the olive oil over medium heat in a sauté pan equipped with a fitted lid. When oil is wavy add the garlic and cook to light brown. Add the broccoli rabe and the salt and toss to coat. Add ½ cup of water and turn the heat to high. Once the water starts to boil cover the pan, reduce heat to medium, and braise the broccoli rabe for 10 minutes. Remove the lid and continue to cook the broccoli rabe until the water has evaporated but the rabe is still moist. Take off heat and set aside.

For the Polenta:

In a small sauce pot bring 4 cups water and
1 teaspoon salt to a boil. Slowly add the corn
meal, stirring constantly. Once the cornmeal is
incorporated reduce the heat to low. Cover and
cook the cornmeal, stirring every 2 to 3 minutes,
for 15 minutes. Add cream and continue to cook
and stir for another 15 minutes. Remove from heat
and stir in the butter and cheese. Cover and set
aside in a warm spot (which at this point should be
anywhere in your kitchen).

For the Fish:

Preheat oven to 400 degrees.

Season the fish with salt and pepper. Place in an
oven-proof pan, drizzle with ¼ cup olive oil and
bake in oven for 12 to 15 minutes.

Arrange 6 mounds of polenta on a platter. Place a
bit of the broccoli rabe at the base of each mound.
Place a piece of swordfish on top of each mound.
Sauce the platter with the Barcaiola sauce.

BROILED SWORDFISH WITH MISO

Serves 2

¾ to 1 pound swordfish steak

2 tablespoons miso (any kind)

2 tablespoons lime juice

1 tablespoon mirin

This is a quick and easy method to cook swordfish in the oven, since many of our customers live in the city and do not have access to a grill.

Whisk miso, lime juice, and mirin together in small bowl. Brush swordfish with the mixture and let marinate for 30 to 45 minutes in the refrigerator. Reserve the leftover miso mixture to use for basting.

Preheat broiler to high. Place swordfish on oiled broiling pan. Depending on the thickness of the swordfish, set oven rack an appropriate distance from broiler (see note on page 25).

Broil 4 to 5 minutes, basting once with miso mixture. Turn fish, baste again and return to broiler and cook until browned, another 4 or 5 minutes, depending on thickness of fish.

WHITING

Whiting, or silver hake, are an abundant local fish. They are not really a "trash" fish but are considered less desirable than cod or sea bass or fluke. We have them fall through the spring at the fish stand, and they usually sell for a fairly low price, around $3.50 per pound.

Alex says that years ago whiting were caught in huge numbers off of Shinnecock in the winter —tens of thousands of pounds. They don't seem to be around in those numbers today but are considered "sustainably managed and responsibly harvested" according to NOAA's FishWatch.

Whiting are small, usually two pounds or under, and are most often sold whole. They are a mild white fish, good to fillet and fry or cook whole. Sometimes whiting is fried and served in a sandwich with hot sauce. In Italy, whiting is referred to as "merluzzi" and used to make a fish soup. When we get a steady supply in season, I like to behead them and smoke them on the bone.

ROAST WHITING WITH TOMATO, ORANGE, AND FENNEL

Serves 2

1 large whole whiting
(or 2 small), 1 to 1 ½ pounds,
gutted and scaled

6 littleneck clams, rinsed

1 medium orange

6 medium tomatoes, peeled,
quartered, seeds removed

1 small fennel bulb, quartered
lengthwise

1 cup clam broth or fish stock

1 cup carrot juice

3 cloves garlic, crushed

1 tablespoon olive oil

1 teaspoon dried basil

1 teaspoon dried sage

Salt and pepper to taste

Preheat oven to 400 degrees.

Zest the orange into a bowl. Put tomatoes, fennel, clam broth and carrot juice in a saucepan. Bring to a boil, then reduce to a simmer.

Add the garlic and the orange zest to the saucepan. Cook until the broth thickens, about 6 to 8 minutes.

Put the whiting in a shallow baking pan. Drizzle with the olive oil and season with the basil, sage, salt and pepper.

Pour the tomato broth over the fish so that the whiting are half-submerged.

Roast in the oven, turning fish after 5 or 6 minutes. Add the clams in their shells over the fish and cook for another 4 minutes or until the clams open and release their broth.

WHITING CHOWDER

Serves 4

2 pounds whole whiting, gutted, skinned and filleted and cut into 1 ½ inch pieces, racks reserved

4 cups water

2 pieces bacon, diced

1 ½ cups chopped leeks, white parts only

2 cups white potatoes, peeled and cut into ½ inch cubes (2 medium potatoes)

2 ½ cups fish stock

2 cups half and half or milk

½ teaspoon salt

¼ teaspoon pepper

2 tablespoons butter

Here whiting is used for both fish stock and chowder; feel free to use any flaky white fish for this savory soup like sea bass, blackfish, cod, or striped bass.

To make fish stock, cover heads, bones and skin of whiting with 4 cups cold water.

Heat to the boiling point then reduce heat to medium-low and simmer for 20 minutes. Strain.

Sauté the bacon in a large pot over medium-low heat until crisp, about 5 minutes. Remove with slotted spoon to a plate lined with paper towels.

Cook leeks in bacon fat and sauté until softened, about 3 to 4 minutes. Add potatoes and fish stock. Turn heat to medium and simmer for 12 minutes until potatoes are tender.

Add the half and half, salt and pepper. Gently add the fish pieces and stir.

Add the butter and the bacon pieces; cover and simmer for 10 minutes. Taste for seasonings and serve hot.

FISH CAKES WITH THREE SAUCES

Makes about 10 Cakes

1 ½ pounds white fish (blackfish, cod, flounder, etc.), trimmed of any bones and cut into large pieces (roughly 3 or 4 inches by 2 inches)

4 to 6 cups water

2 bay leaves

10 peppercorns

3 sprigs fresh parsley

3 sprigs fresh oregano

5 medium potatoes, peeled

½ cup red onion, diced

½ cup chopped fresh parsley

2 tablespoons Old Bay seasoning

2 eggs

1 cup breadcrumbs

½ to ⅓ cup olive oil

At our house we make fish cakes when we get stuck with a couple of pounds of leftover white fish. We've used flounder, fluke, cod or scrod to make cakes to freeze for a quick meal.

Admittedly these fish cakes are very simple —fish, potatoes, onions, herbs and spices. Feel free to add other ingredients of your choice. Fish cakes appear in many cultures with a wide range of ingredients: peas, bacon, rum, corn, coconut butter, etc. You may choose to add lemon, mustard, Thai curry paste, whatever you like.

These may be made with salt cod (which must be soaked) or salmon. They may be rolled in crushed cornflakes, panko, breadcrumbs, or cracker crumbs.

Here is our basic recipe, along with a few different sauces for serving. To freeze the cakes, put one or two in a heavy duty Ziploc bag and keep in the freezer for when you need a quick meal. Just defrost, roll in some breadcrumbs and sauté.

Fill a large frying pan with 3 or 4 inches of water. Warm over medium heat. Add bay leaves, peppercorns, parsley and oregano sprigs.

When water is simmering add the fish. Cover and turn the heat to low. Simmer for 4 minutes. Check fish with a thin-bladed knife to see if it is cooked through. Remove fish with a slotted spoon to a plate; let cool.

Meanwhile fill a medium pot with water and bring to a boil. Add the potatoes and cook until soft, about 20 minutes. Remove with a slotted spoon to a large bowl. Mash the potatoes with a fork or a potato masher; let cool.

To the potatoes add the onion, parsley, Old Bay, eggs and the flaked fish. Gently combine with a wooden spoon or your hands; mixture should be fairly moist.

Put the breadcrumbs in a shallow bowl. Gently cover the cakes with breadcrumbs, shake any excess off and remove to a plate. Continue until you have made all the fish mixture into cakes.

Heat the olive oil in a large frying pan over medium heat. Fry the cakes until golden brown, about 4 minutes per side. Try to flip the cakes only once.

Serve one or two cakes per person with your choice of sauce.

CLASSIC TARTAR SAUCE

1 cup mayonnaise

⅓ cup chopped dill pickles

2 tablespoons Dijon mustard

2 tablespoons pickle juice

Black pepper to taste

Combine all ingredients and mix well. Taste and adjust seasoning.

CHILI LIME SAUCE

3 tablespoons chopped scallions

2 tablespoons prepared chili garlic sauce

2 tablespoons lime juice

2 tablespoons water

1 to 1 ½ tablespoons brown sugar

Combine all ingredients and mix well. Taste and adjust seasoning.

YOGURT DILL SAUCE

½ cup plain yogurt

2 tablespoons chopped fresh dill

1 tablespoon lemon juice

½ teaspoon salt

Combine all ingredients and mix well. Taste and adjust seasoning.

SINGAPOREAN STYLE SEAFOOD STEW

1 pound mussels, debearded and rinsed

1 dozen clams, small size

8 blue crabs, chopped in half (optional)

6 blowfish tails or 1 pound monkfish, cut into chunks

8 large shrimp, peeled

½ cup canola oil

3 tablespoons chopped shallot

3 tablespoons chopped garlic

3 tablespoons chopped lemongrass

1 tablespoon chopped galangal

2 tablespoons chili paste

10 kaffir lime leaves, shredded

1 cup chopped canned tomato with its juice

1 tablespoon annatto oil (optional)

3 cups water

2 tablespoons fish sauce

1 tablespoon sugar

2 tablespoons fresh lime juice

2 tablespoons chopped fresh cilantro

Recipe by Chef Simpson Wong
Chomp Chomp, New York City

Adding crab to this spicy stew makes a thick, robust broth. Galangal is also called "blue ginger," which can be found in most Asian grocery stores. You may substitute regular ginger if you cannot find it.

Heat oil in a large pot over medium-low heat. Add shallot, garlic, lemongrass and galangal to pot. Cook until fragrant.

Add chili paste, kaffir lime leaves, tomato with its juice and annatto oil (if using). Add the water and bring to a boil; reduce heat and let simmer for 5 minutes.

Add mussels, clams and blue crabs (if using). When the mussels and clams open, add the fish and shrimp; stir until the seafood is well-coated with sauce.

Add fish sauce, sugar, and lime juice and stir. Taste and adjust seasonings.

Sprinkle chopped cilantro on top and serve.

Note: Annatto oil comes from heating annatto seed in oil for a few minutes. The oil takes on a crimson red color; the seed is discarded.

FISH FRY ON THE EXPRESSWAY

When I first started driving into the city by myself to do the market, I drove Alex's old van. He's always had regular Ford 250 vans, but this one was an extended cab, a big, gray monster that he bought second hand. Alex liked to joke that he had a gray van so that he could easily repair it with duct tape. To pack everything needed for the fish stand, you had to climb inside, your head against the ceiling and the ripe stench of fish in your nose, and twist and turn coolers and buckets to make them fit.

When you live and work in New York City there's a constant tension on the road: everyone's in a hurry. When you're a pedestrian, you hate vehicles; when you're driving a vehicle, you hate pedestrians —that's the recipe that makes walking and driving in the city such a competitive, high stress endeavor. At first I was apprehensive about driving a big vehicle by myself in New York, but driving the exact same route week after week lent me confidence. Trucking on the Long Island Expressway (otherwise known as Long Island's biggest parking lot), through the Midtown Tunnel, and downtown to Union Square, I soon got over my nerves and the comfortable feeling of routine set in.

I leave Mattituck early, about 4 am —early enough to avoid most problems getting into the city. One Wednesday morning, I was on my way to the market with an especially full load. We had upgraded from a van to a big box truck, and it was October: prime time for fishing. About an hour into my trip, I saw smoke coming from the engine. We'd been having some radiator problems, and assuming it was overheating again, I pulled over on the side of the road and called Alex. It was one of the many moments I've found myself thankful for the existence of cellphones —like times when Alex called from the boat to say he would be out fishing later than normal or was at the dock trying to repair a net; at least I knew he was okay. Now I was phoning him from the side of the road, letting him know I was okay, but there was a problem. "What kind of problem?" he said. "Where are you?" I was telling him the truck had overheated when I turned around to find the cab filled with smoke.

"Yikes!" I said into the phone. "It's on fire!" I grabbed a small fire extinguisher and popped the hood. The entire engine compartment was blazing. Tiny extinguisher aimed and ready, I unloaded its contents onto the fire, ten seconds of firefighting to little avail. Gagging and coughing from the smoke, I called 911 and had a really nasty exchange with the operator, who wanted to know my exact location, but I couldn't see the sign on the expressway. What exit was I near? I yelled "My truck is burning up, send the fire department!" It was about that time that I realized that there were two gas tanks in the truck, and maybe I should get the hell out of there.

I grabbed my money bag for the market, my coat, and cell phone. Then I ran. I stood down the road watching the truck burn, expecting a fire truck to show up any second. While I waited a trucker going the opposite direction on the Expressway pulled over. There were six lanes and a concrete barrier between us. He waved to signal me. I waved my cellphone so he knew I'd called the fire department. There was not much that he could do, so he drove on. When the firemen finally arrived, the truck was fully engulfed.

After the adrenaline rush subsided, a Nassau county police officer rolled up. I was crying, and he did his best to calm me down and let me wait in his cruiser until Alex got there. It turned out the firefighters were late because they'd been fighting a fire all night at a local dairy that had burned to the ground. Exhausted, covered with soot, with tired eyes they slumped through the job. One of them saw a whole flounder that had fallen out of a cooler and asked me if he could have it so he could play a prank on his boss by putting it on his chair. I just looked at him. "Sure," I said, unable to find my sense of humor. He picked up the flounder and walked away grinning.

Once the fire burned out, a tow truck hauled the remains to a junkyard. Alex and I tried to scavenge some tools or equipment, but anything recognizable was fused to the truck body. In the end we walked away with only the license plates.

Talk about a bad morning. We called the Greenmarket managers in Manhattan and let them know what happened. One of them stood in our spot for a few hours relaying the bad news to the customers. Alex and I spent the next few days replacing all of our equipment so that we could do our Saturday market. When we got to market that Saturday some of the customers were asking what happened to us on Wednesday.

"Didn't you hear?" I said. "Our truck caught fire on the way in." "What?" the man said. "Your truck burned up?" For a moment he didn't seem to believe me, then he put it together in his head. "Oh!" he said. "I did hear about that on the radio. They said, 'Fish fry on the expressway!'"

FLOUNDER

We catch several different types of flounder in Long Island that we sell at different times of the year —fluke (summer flounder), blackback (winter flounder), yellowtail, and sand dabs. There are additional lesser-known types of local flatfish with great names like hogchoker (they are small and fat and were supposedly fed to the pigs) and windowpane flounder or daylights (when held up to the light they are so thin you can see daylight through them).

Different types of flatfish are caught at different times of the year as the fish migrate. Fluke is common in the summer and fall and is thicker and firmer than other types of flatfish; it is ideal for sashimi. It is popular with both recreational and commercial fishermen and is tightly controlled by state and federal regulations. The fluke stocks are considered rebuilt and not overfished.

Blackback flounder have thin, soft fillets, and are not suitable to eat raw. Their flavor is delicate and mild. Blackbacks are heavily regulated, and they are pretty scarce these days; they are also called lemon sole. As we see more striped bass around we have noticed less winter flounder. When striped bass are cleaned you can often find winter flounder in their bellies.

Yellowtail flounder have thin, delicate, yellowish fillets. Yellowtail stocks are below target population levels and are currently under a rebuilding plan.

American plaice, or sand dabs, are a cold-water species of flounder that we generally only see in the winter. According to NOAA's 2015 Assessment Report, the catch data show that the stock is not overfished and overfishing is not occurring.

Some general flatfish rules: use fluke if you want to eat raw flatfish; other types of flounder are too soft. Thick pieces of fluke are also ideal for baking or broiling in the oven. Smaller, softer fillets are better to pan fry or steam. Roast, pan fry, or salt bake any type of whole flounder.

FLOUNDER WITH BUTTER AND HERB SAUCE

Serves 2

1 pound flounder fillets

¼ cup all-purpose flour

Salt and pepper to taste

3 tablespoons butter

1 tablespoon olive oil

2 tablespoons white wine

3 tablespoons chopped fresh sage, parsley or chives

Lemon wedges

Put the flour in a small bowl. Season the flounder fillets with salt and pepper, then dredge them in the flour and set aside on a plate.

In a large skillet, heat the butter and the oil over medium heat, shaking the pan back and forth to integrate. Add the white wine and raise the heat to medium-high.

Add the fillets to the skillet and cook for 2 to 3 minutes; turn the fillets and cook for another 2 to 3 minutes depending on their thickness. Remove the fillets from the pan and put on a plate.

If all of the fish did not fit in the skillet, cook the rest of the fish, adding another tablespoon of butter to the pan if necessary. Remove to a plate.

Add the herbs to the remaining pan sauce. Using medium-low heat, stir the herbs in the pan sauce for 2 minutes, then pour the sauce over the fillets. Serve with lemon wedges.

FLOUNDER WITH MUSHROOM TARRAGON SAUCE

Serves 2

1 pound flounder fillets

3 tablespoons butter

3 tablespoons olive oil

¼ cup minced shallots

1 large clove garlic, chopped

2 cups chopped mushrooms
(any kind, or use a blend of
baby bella, shitake, or oyster
mushrooms)

Salt and pepper to taste

½ cup white wine

1 tablespoon finely chopped
fresh tarragon

¼ cup heavy cream

In a deep skillet, heat the butter and oil over medium heat while shaking the pan back and forth to integrate. Add the shallots to the pan and cook until softened, stirring occasionally. Add the garlic and cook for 1 minute, then add the mushrooms and cook for 6 to 9 minutes until they've released their water and softened. Add salt and pepper to taste.

Stir in the wine and simmer for 2 minutes.

Meanwhile, oil a non-stick skillet and cook the flounder fillets over medium heat, 2 minutes per side.

While the flounder fillets are cooking, turn the heat under the mushroom sauce to low. Stir in the tarragon and the cream.

When the sauce is heated thoroughly, distribute it over the flounder fillets and serve.

FLOUNDER "A LA PLANCHA" WITH CATALONIAN EGGPLANT RELISH

Serves 4

4 (4-ounce) flounder or fluke fillets

3 large Japanese eggplants, cut into ½ inch-thick rounds (4 cups total)

Olive oil cooking spray

Salt

1 teaspoon extra-virgin olive oil

1 tablespoon chopped garlic

¼ cup toasted almonds, chopped

Pinch of crushed red pepper flakes

1 cup small-diced green bell peppers

1 cup no-salt-added crushed tomatoes

¼ cup golden raisins

Dash of cinnamon

Dash of smoked paprika

Dash of ground coriander

Lemon wedges, for serving

Recipe by Chef/Author Rocco DiSpirito from *The Negative Calorie Diet*, 2016

In Spain, seafood is often cooked a la plancha, which means that it is cooked simply and quickly, over high heat on a griddle. This Spanish-inspired dish incorporates aromatic Spanish spices with a Catalan-style eggplant relish. It is truly negative calorie food at its best and most flavorful!

For a truly authentic touch, try adding an anchovy fillet to the skillet once the garlic has browned.

Preheat the oven to 400 degrees. Spread the eggplant out on a rimmed baking sheet, and spray the eggplant with cooking spray. Season it with salt and bake in the oven until browned and soft, 5 to 7 minutes. Remove from the oven and set aside.

Pour the olive oil into a large nonstick skillet and place it over medium-high heat. Add the garlic and cook until golden brown, about 2 minutes. Add the chopped toasted almonds, red pepper flakes, and bell peppers, and cook until soft, 2 to 3 minutes. Add the tomatoes, raisins, and eggplant, and cook until everything is sticking to the eggplant as sauce would stick to pasta. Season with salt and the spices; set the relish aside and keep warm.

Place a cast-iron skillet over high heat. Spray the fish with cooking spray and season with salt. Place the fish in the hot skillet and cook until seared on both sides, about 1 minute per side. Place 1 fillet on each of four plates. Spoon eggplant relish onto the plate and serve with lemon wedges.

FLOUNDER IN SAOR

Serves 4

2 pounds flounder fillets, cut in 2 to 3 inch pieces, trimmed of all bones

½ cup canola oil

1 cup all-purpose flour

Salt to taste

½ cup olive oil

3 cups thinly sliced white onions

½ cup red wine vinegar

⅓ cup pine nuts

⅓ cup golden raisins

Saor is a classic Venetian recipe for cooked, then pickled fish. Sardines or mackerel are traditionally used; this one is done with flounder. We use the slightly ragged pieces of flounder left over from a day at the fish stand that are unsuitable to sell.

We were introduced to this dish by a customer that invited us over for Thanksgiving appetizers. It was so good that we stood by the plate and unashamedly ate most of it! She passed on her recipe, which was from Marcella's Italian Kitchen by Marcella Hazan.

This is my version of Flounder in Saor; *there are many variations of this recipe available. I like lots of onions, and the pine nuts and raisins are a must.*

Heat the oil in a large frying pan. Dredge the flounder pieces in the flour and coat well on both sides. Fry the flounder pieces to a golden brown color, a few minutes on each side. Remove flounder to a plate lined with paper towels.

Season flounder liberally with the salt. Layer the plate with more paper towels, and continue to fry and salt all the remaining fish.

In a separate frying pan, heat the ½ cup of olive oil over medium-low heat. Add the onion, and cook for about 20 minutes until the onion is a light brown color.

Turn off the heat and add the vinegar to the pan; stir. Let cool slightly.

Put the fish in a large rectangular Tupperware container or a glass baking dish. Pour the onions and vinegar gently over the fish. Scatter the pine nuts and raisins on top.

Cover the container and refrigerate overnight. This dish is best after marinating at least one whole day.

To serve, bring to room temperature.

FLUKE EN CROUTE WITH SAUCE PROPOSAL AND ROMANESCO

Serves 4

For the Sauce Proposal:

10 ounces (20 tablespoons) unsalted butter

¼ cup hazelnuts

Olive oil

½ Vidalia onion, brunoise

3 tablespoons Romanesco florets or regular cauliflower florets

Kosher salt

½ cup fresh lime juice

½ cup low-sodium soy sauce

3 tablespoons golden raisins

2 tablespoons chopped capers

2 tablespoons chopped fresh curly parsley

1 tablespoon red pepper flakes

For the Cauliflower Puree:

4 cups roughly chopped cauliflower

3 cups heavy cream

Pinch of kosher salt

For the Fluke:

4 (4-ounce) fluke fillets, skin removed

1 large egg white

2 tablespoons chopped fresh curly parsley

1 teaspoon red pepper flakes

4 (¼-inch-thick) slices Pullman loaf (see Note)

Extra-virgin olive oil

Kosher salt

Freshly ground black pepper

Recipe by Chef/Author Marc Forgione, Restaurant Marc Forgione, American Cut, Khe-Yo, New York City

For the Sauce Proposal:

Make the brown butter: Add 4 tablespoons of the butter to a sauté pan set over medium heat and cook until the solids brown, 3 to 5 minutes. Immediately transfer the brown butter to an ice bath, whisking to cool down the butter. This step is important because if the brown butter is not whisked while being cooled, it will separate. Refrigerate until ready to use.

Preheat the oven to 350 degrees; position the rack in the middle. Toast the hazelnuts in a shallow baking pan for 10 to 12 minutes, or until fragrant. Remove the skins by rubbing the hazelnuts with a kitchen towel. Cool the nuts, then place them in a plastic bag. Using a mallet or a rolling pin, pound the nuts until they are crushed. Set aside 2 tablespoons; reserve the rest for another use (or eat them!).

Add enough olive oil to a sauté pan to cover the bottom of the pan and set it over low heat. Add the onion and cook, stirring from time to time, until translucent, 3 to 4 minutes. Remove from the heat and set aside.

Add enough olive oil to a sauté pan to cover the bottom of the pan and set it over high heat. Just before the oil starts to smoke, add enough raw florets to cover the bottom of the pan in one layer (you may need to do this in batches), reduce the heat to medium, and cook for 2 to 3 minutes. Once the florets begin to brown slightly, add 3 tablespoons of the butter. Let the butter melt, gently shake the pan, season with salt, and transfer the florets to a plate lined with a paper towel. Repeat with the remaining florets. Set the cooked florets aside.

In a 2-quart saucepan, bring the lime juice and soy sauce to a boil. Reduce the heat to low and gradually whisk in the remaining 3 tablespoons butter, 1 tablespoon at a time, until well incorporated and emulsified. Whisk in the reserved brown butter, 1 tablespoon at a time. Remove from the heat and blend with an immersion blender or in a stand blender. Keep the sauce warm.

Right before serving, stir in the cooked florets, raisins, capers, parsley, and red pepper flakes.

For the Cauliflower Puree:

In a saucepot, combine the cauliflower, cream, and a pinch of salt, and cook over medium heat until the cauliflower is cooked through, about 25 minutes. Reserve the cooking liquid. Transfer the cauliflower to a food processor fitted with a blade, or a blender, and pulse a few times. Add the cooking liquid, a couple of tablespoons at a time, until the mixture is smooth and light. If you add too much cooking liquid too fast, your blender might explode, so be sure to add it slowly.

For the Fluke en Croute:

Preheat the oven to 350 degrees; position the rack in the middle. Rinse and pat the fish dry. Brush one side of the fillets with the egg white. Sprinkle the parsley and red pepper flakes over the egg white side. Lay the bread slices out and place the fillets over the bread, herb-side down. Trim the bread to fit the fillets, and gently flip the fish over so that the bread is on top.

Add enough oil to a large skillet to cover the bottom of the pan and set it over medium heat. Season two of the fillets with salt and pepper and add them to the pan, bread-side down. Carefully watch the fish, and once the edges begin to brown, transfer the fish to a Silpat- or parchment paper–lined baking pan, bread-side up. Pour the oil from the pan on top of the fish. Repeat with the remaining fillets. Let the fillets sit out for 5 minutes together so they are all roughly the same temperature when they go into the oven. Bake the fish for about 4 minutes, or until a cake tester, when inserted into the fish, comes out without any force.

Divide the fish among 4 warmed plates. Spoon the Cauliflower Puree on the side and liberally drizzle the sauce over the fish.

Note: For better results freeze the Pullman loaf before slicing.

SALT-BAKED WHOLE FLUKE

Serves 2 to 4

1 whole fluke, 2 to 3 pounds, gutted but not scaled

4 to 5 cups kosher salt

Water

Lemon wedges

This is a joyfully simple recipe: a fish covered in a salt crust and then baked. The crust hardens and causes the fish to slowly steam, resulting in moist, delicate flesh. If you do a little research you will find lots of recipes calling for the addition of egg whites and herbs to the salt and the cavity stuffed with citrus and herbs. Feel free to experiment with those ingredients, but it is fine to prepare this dish with just salt. You won't be disappointed.

Use any smallish whole fish, like porgy, sea bass, sea trout, flounder, or fluke. It is not necessary for the fish to be scaled, as the scales will be pulled away with the salt when the crust is broken.

This makes a great presentation for your guests when you crack and remove the crust from the fish. The smell released is divine.

Preheat oven to 425 degrees.

In a large bowl mix the salt with a bit of water —it should feel like wet sand. On a rimmed baking sheet large enough to hold the fish, make a bed of salt large enough for the fish. Place the gutted fish on the bed of salt and cover the fish completely with the salt mixture.

Bake for 25 to 30 minutes. Remove from oven and let cool for 10 minutes.

Crack the crust and brush the salt aside; the scales and skin should come off with the salt, but you may have to peel it back. Remove the top fillets and serve a portion to each person. Lift the backbone of the fish and remove the bottom fillets. Serve with a squeeze of fresh lemon.

CRISPY FLOUNDER WITH ONION AGRO DOLCE

Serves 6

For the Agro Dolce:

¼ cup extra virgin olive oil

1 pound red onions, peeled, root cut off and thinly sliced lengthwise

2 teaspoons salt

10 twists fresh black pepper

¼ cup red wine

1 sprig rosemary, 3 inches long

1 bay leaf

2 tablespoons superfine sugar

¼ cup dried cherries

½ cup + 1 tablespoon red wine vinegar

For the Fish:

1 ½ pounds flounder fillet

2 cups flour

2 eggs beaten with 1 tablespoon water

3 cups bread crumbs

Salt and pepper

2 cups vegetable oil

1 tablespoon chopped fresh parsley

Recipe by Chef Carmen Quagliata, Union Square Cafe, New York City

For the Agro Dolce:

In a large sauté pan over medium-high heat, heat the oil and add onions. Season with salt and pepper. Stir to break up onions and press down lightly. Once onions start to brown, add wine, rosemary, and bay leaf, and reduce to almost dry. Add the sugar, cherries, and ½ cup of the vinegar. Continue to simmer over medium-high heat, cook down until compote and liquid is syrupy.

Remove from heat and finish with 1 tablespoon vinegar. Transfer to a bowl, allow to cool and serve at room temperature. Keep the agro dolce refrigerated, covered well, up to a week.

For the Fish:

Set up a standard breading procedure in 3 wide deep plates. Fill 1 with flour, 1 with the beaten eggs, and 1 with the breadcrumbs.

Cut the flounder into 6 pieces on the bias, season with salt and pepper. Bread the fish by dredging lightly in the flour, then the egg wash, then the bread crumbs. Lay breaded fish on a baking sheet and refrigerate until needed.

Heat the oil in a large sauté pan over high heat until wavy and very hot. Gently place the fish in the pan and fry for 1 minute on both sides. It should be golden brown. Place the fish on a platter and spoon a tablespoon of the Agro Dolce over each piece of fish. Sprinkle the platter with the parsley.

FLOUNDER ROE

Roe from different types of fish are eaten all over the world. The flounder roe that we sell is very mild-tasting and comes in a pair of delicate orange egg sacs, much like shad roe. We have it in season from late fall through early spring.

Many folks are surprised to find that flounder roe does not consist of large round eggs, like the salmon roe you'd find in a sushi restaurant. These sacs are dense with tiny eggs and must be cooked through, but not so much that it gets too dry. Roe can be pan fried, broiled, or used to thicken soups.

PAN-FRIED FLOUNDER ROE

Serves 2

4 pieces roe (about ¾ to 1 pound)

Salt and pepper

½ cup flour

2 tablespoons butter

Lemon wedges

This is our go-to flounder roe recipe. We like it with eggs for breakfast.

Season the roe with salt and pepper. Put the flour in a shallow bowl and gently dredge the roe in it; shake off any excess flour.

Heat a pan over medium heat and melt the butter. Sauté the roe until golden brown, about 3 minutes. Gently turn the roe and cook another 1 minute. Do not overcook.

Serve with lemon wedges.

JOHN DORY

John Dory is a mysterious fish that we do not have very often —of course that means customers are eager to get it. It is mostly caught as a bycatch here in the Western Atlantic, and is caught offshore in deep water. Some years we have quite a bit in the summer, and some years none at all.

John Dory looks like a big, silvery butterfish. Viewed from the side it looks like a regular fish; viewed from the front it is narrow. Its flattened appearance is somewhat strange. It's also known as St. Peter's fish (St. Peter is the patron saint of fishermen).

At the fish stand we describe dory as a white fish, buttery, and flavorful, and maybe a touch oily. The fillets are firm and will stand up to grilling. If you see it available, try it, it doesn't come around that often.

GRILLED JOHN DORY FILLET

Serves 4

2 pounds John Dory fillet

¼ cup Worcestershire sauce

2 limes, juiced

1 teaspoon salt

Mix the Worcestershire sauce, lime juice, and salt together in a bowl.

Place fillets in a glass or plastic container with a lid and pour the marinade over the fish. Turn the fish a few times so it is completely coated. Marinate for 30 to 45 minutes under refrigeration.

Grill for 3 to 4 minutes per side.

SKATE

Skates are similar to stingrays and are abundant locally. There is a lot of misinformation out there that says skate is overfished, but that is not true. According to the New England Fishery Management Council, "overfishing is not occurring on any of the seven" species of skate in the Northeast.

Alex says that at times very small skates are so abundant that they are considered pests. At other times of year, when they are larger, they can be sold cheaply or used as lobster bait.

A few years ago Alex brought up a stingray (different from a skate) in his net that was estimated to be 250 to 300 pounds. He had to call another fisherman over to his boat; they built a ramp and were able to push the ray overboard safely.

Customers often mention the rumor that some fishmongers stamp out round pieces of skate and try to pass them off as scallops. We do not know of anyone who has actually done that; skate is stringy and not similar in texture to a scallop at all.

Skate meat is very sweet, almost like crabmeat, and has a ridged texture. It's commonly sold in thin fillets that have been cut off the cartilage, and sometimes sold on the "bone" —a layer of meat on the top and bottom and a piece of cartilage in between. We used to sell skate on the bone at the fish stand until the special planing machine used for skinning the skate pieces broke and could not be repaired. If you buy skate on the bone, cook it with the bone in and pull the meat off with a fork. Cook skate no later than the day after you buy it.

SKATE SALAD

Serves 2 to 4

1 pound skate fillet

4 cups water

¼ cup white wine vinegar

½ lemon cut into half-moons

5 to 6 sprigs thyme

2 bay leaves

10 peppercorns

For the Vinaigrette:

3 tablespoons olive oil

2 tablespoons white wine vinegar

1 tablespoon minced garlic

2 teaspoons stone-ground mustard

½ teaspoon salt

Freshly ground pepper to taste

For the Salad:

½ cup diced carrot

¼ cup diced scallions

¼ cup chopped Kalamata olives

2 tablespoons chopped fresh parsley

2 tablespoons chopped fresh basil

Basil sprigs for garnish

Greens or Cooked Rice (optional)

This tender salad can be made with poached, pan-fried, or steamed skate. If you use skate on the bone instead of fillets, cook for a bit longer, about 10 minutes.

Trim the skate fillets of any skin or pieces of cartilage. Put a deep skillet on medium heat and add the water and the vinegar, lemon, thyme, bay leaves and peppercorns.

When water is steaming and starting to bubble, add the skate fillets and cover. Cook for 3 to 4 minutes. Remove the fillets to a plate with a slotted spoon and set aside.

To make the vinaigrette, whisk olive oil, white wine vinegar, garlic, mustard, salt and pepper together.

Flake the skate fillets apart and put in a large bowl. Add the carrot, scallions, olives, parsley, and basil. Add the vinaigrette and gently combine.

Serve the salad as is, or over rice or greens. Garnish with basil sprigs.

SKATE IN BROWN BUTTER SAUCE

Serves 2

1 pound skate fillet
(2 or 3 pieces)

Salt and pepper

¼ cup all-purpose flour

2 tablespoons olive oil

4 tablespoons butter

1 tablespoon lemon juice

1 tablespoon capers, drained

1 tablespoon chopped fresh
parsley

Season the skate fillets with salt and pepper and dredge in the flour.

Warm a nonstick skillet over medium heat and add the olive oil to the pan. When a pinch of flour added to the pan sizzles, add the skate fillets and cook for 3 minutes. Turn fillets carefully and cook for another 3 minutes. Remove to a warm plate.

Wipe out the pan with a paper towel. Turn the heat to medium-low and add butter to the pan; cook for 2 minutes until butter turns light brown.

Take the pan off the heat and add the lemon juice, capers, and parsley; stir well. Pour sauce over the skate and serve.

ROSIE

This is one of the more bizarre but true Blue Moon stories. I got a call from Alex one Saturday morning at six a.m., "Uh, Steph?" he said. "Rosie's lost in Prospect Park."

Rosie is our cat.

Just before Alex leaves for our Saturday markets around 3:45 a.m., he opens the back of the truck to put a few last-minute things inside. Usually he has to go back into the house to get the menu signs and a few clean buckets. Rosie must have jumped up into the back of the truck while he was inside. When he came back out, he shut the door and drove into the city. He was stuck in traffic on the BQE with no idea Rosie was riding in the back. When he got to Grand Army Plaza, he opened the back of the truck and Rosie came flying out and took off like a shot into the park.

So Ruby and I dragged ourselves out of bed that morning, got dressed, and drove into Brooklyn to search for her.

It was Memorial Day weekend, and Prospect Park was gearing up for a weekend full of barbecue grills, lawn games, and holiday revelers. Some of the farmers and customers helped us search the bushes and wooded areas for Rosie, but she was likely terrified and hiding. We couldn't find her; she was gone. To top it off, Ruby and I returned from the long search to find my car had been towed.

The hunt continued for months. We had "Lost Cat" signs at the fish stand. People began posting sightings of her on our Facebook page. I called local friends to go check out each tip, and, eager to help, they would hurry to the park, but Rosie was never there.

The weather got hotter; muggy and tropical, as only August in New York City can be. I thought of her hiding in the bushes with no water. I wandered for miles in the park, sweating, searching for her —did you know that Prospect Park is 585 acres? In my over twenty years of working at the Grand Army Plaza Greenmarket, I had rarely even gone into the park, much less had time to explore it. I scoured areas that I had never been in before: twisting trails through giant trees where I hardly saw another soul, and places where homeless people stored their possessions. I trekked past playgrounds, the lake, the bandshell. I saw countless bikers and joggers and ran into a few customers walking their dogs. They promised to keep an eye out for Rosie, and one of them warned me about walking near the Three

Fountains area, a notorious cruising section of the park. "You'll probably be okay," she said, as she walked off with her dog.

One night I got a call from a guy who insisted that he had found Rosie. "A tabby with a pink collar is sitting on Plaza Street looking at me," he said. So I drove into Brooklyn on a Saturday night with an empty cat carrier in the back of my car, heading for the address he gave me. Brooklyn was jumping at 11 p.m., with souped-up cars, loud music, and people dressed to the nines —the polar opposite of Mattituck. I found the address and found the cat! It was a tabby with a pink collar . . . but it was not Rosie.

Months went by. The market season ended. The winter was cold with lots of freezing, below zero mornings. We arrived in Florida for our winter respite just as New York City was about to be hit by an enormous blizzard. Then Alex's sister called. She had been contacted by a Brooklyn animal hospital that had received a lost cat and scanned its microchip. It was Rosie!

My six year old was ready to get in the car and drive fifteen hundred miles to Brooklyn to get her. When I told her we couldn't do that, she offered to get on a plane by herself, fly to New York, pick Rosie up and bring her back home. "No problem, Mom!"

Rosie had somehow found her way into the basement of the Brooklyn Public Library, across a very busy street from the park. We got a call from a very nice lady who was the library's artist-in-residence. She was doing a photography project in the library basement and saw that the custodian was leaving food out for a cat he was trying to catch. As she left the library one day she happened to see the custodian with a cat in a trap. She did a good deed and took the cat to One Love Animal Hospital instead of to a shelter.

Rosie must have been living on small rodents and the custodian's cat food, and drinking out of toilets in the library (at least that's the habit she had when she came home).

She was very skinny and dehydrated, and she recovered in the animal hospital for a few days until we could get some friends to take her in. She did well with them and their two year old, except for routinely waking them up every day at four in the morning —that's when the fisherman gets up; talk about a rude awakening!

When the news got back to all of our friends and customers, they were ecstatic. Someone from WNYC did a story on the radio and wrote it up for their website; when I shared it online it went viral, receiving about 15,000 views. Why, I wondered, did so many people care about us finding our lost cat? Well, everyone loves a happy ending!

Rosie is still with us and is still a wanderer, although she doesn't stay out as much as she used to. She is delighted to lie in a cozy bed or in front of the fire. And these days we are careful to keep her inside until the fish truck pulls out of the driveway.

FLAVORFUL FISH

BLUEFISH

Anyone who fishes on the East Coast, recreationally or commercially, knows bluefish. Strong fighting fish, they are fun and challenging to catch, though their razor sharp teeth can easily bite off a finger. About 70 percent of the total bluefish catch is caught annually by recreational fisherman. Here on Long Island, kids learn to fish by catching snapper blues (very small bluefish around 8 to 10 inches long) in the summer.

Blues are known for their dark, rich, oily meat, containing the omega-3 fatty acids that are so nutritious. The one caveat is they must be very fresh, as the oil in the flesh turns rancid rapidly.

At the fish stand, I find that people who don't like blue have never had a really fresh piece. We sell fresh fillets, caught within one day and immediately iced, and they are delicious. Blues have a hardcore, cult-like following at the fish stand; we have several customers that make ceviche with them.

Blue has soft flaky flesh like codfish, so I like to bake or broil it. Whatever way you make it, it's excellent cooked with something acidic to cut the oil, like lemon, lime, or tomato. Blue can be kept a day after you buy it, but it is best to cook it right away.

BLUEFISH WITH GIN AND LIME

Serves 2

1 bluefish fillet, ¾ to 1 pound

1 medium onion, sliced

1 large carrot, peeled and cut in pieces

1 tablespoon olive oil

Salt and pepper

1 small lime, juiced

2 tablespoons butter, cut in 4 pieces

½ cup gin

2 teaspoons fresh thyme leaves

Set oven to 425 degrees.

Put the onions and carrots in a single layer in a baking dish. Toss with the olive oil and season with salt and pepper.

Bake for 18 to 20 minutes until the onions and carrots are softened.

Remove from the oven and lay the bluefish fillet on top of the onions and carrots. Pour the lime juice over the fish and season with salt and pepper.

Arrange the butter on top of the fish. Pour the gin over the fish and sprinkle with the thyme.

Bake for 8 to 10 minutes, depending on the thickness of the fish. Check with a thin-bladed knife to see if the fish is cooked through.

Serve with the sauce and the vegetables spooned over the fish.

BROILED BLUEFISH WITH LEMON, CAPERS, AND MUSTARD

Serves 2

1 pound bluefish fillet

1 tablespoon olive oil

1 red onion, sliced

2 cloves garlic, crushed

2 teaspoons Dijon mustard

1 lemon, cut in half, with one half cut into half-moons

1 teaspoon capers

1 to 2 tablespoons chopped fresh parsley

Set broiler to high (see note on page 25). Brush a baking sheet or shallow baking dish with the olive oil.

Add the onion and garlic. Broil for about 6 minutes, until the onions and garlic are softened.

Remove pan from broiler; place the fish on top of the onions and garlic.

Spread the mustard over the fish. Squeeze half of the lemon over the fish. Place the lemon slices over top of the fish and sprinkle with the capers.

Broil for about 10 minutes, depending on the thickness of the fish.

Remove from oven and sprinkle with the chopped parsley.

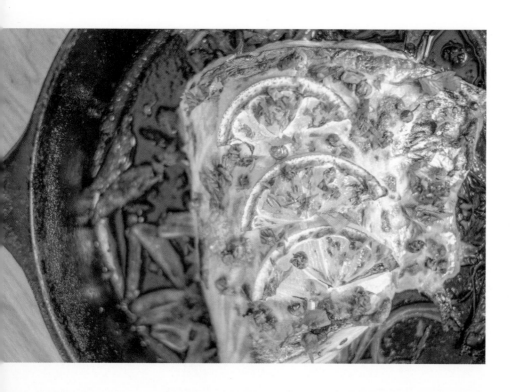

SMOKED BLUEFISH DIP, 3 WAYS

Serves 4 as an Appetizer

Smoked Bluefish I
(with Cream Cheese)

4 ounces (8 tablespoons) smoked bluefish, broken into chunks, bones and skin removed

4 ounces (8 tablespoons) cream cheese

3 tablespoons chopped scallions

1 tablespoon chopped fresh dill

3 teaspoons lemon juice

Smoked Bluefish II
(with Crème Fraîche)

4 ounces (8 tablespoons) smoked bluefish, broken into chunks, bones and skin removed

4 ounces (8 tablespoons) crème fraîche

1 tablespoon chopped fresh chives

1 tablespoon chopped fresh parsley

2 teaspoons lemon juice

1 teaspoon horseradish

Smoked Bluefish III
(with Mayonnaise)

4 ounces (8 tablespoons) smoked bluefish, broken into chunks, bones and skin removed

2 ounces (4 tablespoons) mayonnaise

1 tablespoon good mustard (German or Dijon)

1 teaspoon chopped fresh thyme

We did a taste test to find the most delicious version of smoked bluefish dip. We used cream cheese, mayonnaise, or crème fraîche as binders, then added different seasonings, as well as lemon, horseradish and fresh herbs. Our team of tasters chose the cream cheese version as the winner, with crème fraîche coming in second place, but try what you like best or what you have around —it's hard to go wrong. Serve the dip with crackers or bread and a squeeze of lemon if you like.

Note: When breaking up the fish, remove any bones or pieces of skin. We prefer to break it up by hand and keep the texture of the dip fairly chunky, but you could put it in a food processor for a smoother texture.

Mix all ingredients. Store in a tightly covered container.

HERRING

Herring are very plentiful, small, schooling fish that serve as food for many marine animals, including sharks, whales, skates, seals, flounder, cod, and seabirds. Here in Eastern Long Island, they are mostly considered bait.

According to a 2015 stock assessment, the spawning stock biomass of Atlantic herring is over three times the target level, and is not overfished or subject to overfishing.

Herring is mostly sold pickled or smoked, but it can be eaten fresh as well. It is very oily, one of the fish highest in healthy omega-3 fatty acids, and contains many small bones that remain even after filleting. Pickling the herring softens the bones noticeably.

Fresh herring is apparently quite hard to find in this country, which is a shame, because it is inexpensive, plentiful, and healthy. We only sold pickled herring at the fish stand for years. Gradually we introduced herring fillets, which were immediately scooped up by European and Japanese customers, who cook it fresh or pickle it. We have eaten it raw and enjoyed it, despite the bones!

RAW HERRING

Serves 2 as an Appetizer

½ pound raw herring fillets
(about 4 to 6 pieces)

3 tablespoons diced red onion

Sea salt

One of our customers, Mark Russ Federman, happens to be the (retired) proprietor of the great appetizing store Russ & Daughters on the Lower East Side. He filled us in on maatjes herring, the first young herring of the season, eaten raw in Holland. It is actually frozen and salted before being eaten with pickles and onions, or on bread.

We decided to try unfrozen, unsalted raw herring one day at the fish stand on a slow day when we weren't selling too much herring fillet. It was simple and delicious, and definitely a healthy snack.

Cut the herring fillets into bite-size pieces and arrange on a plate. Sprinkle with the red onion and the sea salt and serve.

PICKLED HERRING

Makes about 8 pints

5 pounds herring fillets

1 pound salt

For the Brine:

2 ½ cups water

2 ½ cups cider vinegar

1 ¼ cups white vinegar

1 pound apples, washed, cored and sliced

1 pound red onions, sliced

3 tablespoons lemon juice

3 tablespoons brown sugar

1 ½ tablespoons Dijon mustard

1 ½ tablespoons celery salt

1 ½ tablespoons ground allspice

1 ½ tablespoons black pepper

1 bay leaf

This is the recipe for our famous pickled herring that we sell at the Greenmarket. We usually do batches of 50 pounds of herring; here the recipe is cut down to a reasonable amount to produce at home. The salting step draws out water from the fillets and firms them up. The pickling brine makes the fine bones in the herring soften and almost disappear. We have also made this with whole herring cleaned, scaled and cut into chunks, leaving the bone in.

In container with a cover, pour the salt over the herring fillets. Mix well with your hands until herring is coated with the salt. Refrigerate for 12 to 24 hours.

Rinse the herring twice under running water. Slice the fillets into 1-inch pieces. Place in a large container with a cover that will fit in your refrigerator.

To make the brine, add all the other ingredients to the herring and mix well. Let the herring marinate in the brine, refrigerated, for 2 to 3 days, stirring once or twice a day.

Pack herring, the onions and apples, and some of the brine into glass or plastic containers. Herring will keep for at least 4 weeks under refrigeration.

PICKLED HERRING WITH CARROT AND LEMON

Makes 1 quart

¾ to 1 pound fresh herring
fillet

½ cup salt

For the Brine:

¾ cups water

¾ cups white vinegar

¼ cup sugar

1 large clove garlic, cut in
quarters

¼ teaspoon ground allspice

¼ teaspoon mustard seed

¼ teaspoon coriander seed

1 bay leaf

1 medium white onion, sliced
(about 1 ¼ cups)

1 medium carrot, peeled and
sliced (about 1 cup)

½ large lemon, sliced into
half-moons

*Here is a slightly different version with fresh lemon and
spices.*

In container with a cover pour the salt over the
herring fillets. Mix well with your hands until herring
is coated with the salt. Refrigerate for 12 to 24 hours.

Rinse the herring twice under running water. Slice
the fillets into 1-inch pieces. Place in a large container
with a cover that will fit in your refrigerator.

In a medium saucepan heat the water, vinegar,
sugar, garlic, and spices over medium heat. When
the liquid boils, turn to a simmer and cook until
sugar is dissolved, stirring occasionally. Remove
from heat and cool.

In a large glass mason jar or plastic container,
layer the herring, onion, carrot and lemon until
the container is full. Pour the cooled brine over
the herring mixture. Cover and let marinate for 2
days. Herring will keep for at least 4 weeks under
refrigeration.

PAN-FRIED HERRING WITH OATMEAL

Serves 2

½ pound herring fillet

Salt and pepper

¾ cup oats

2 teaspoons mustard, any kind

3 tablespoons vegetable oil

An elderly Scottish customer told me that she used to eat herring cooked this way as a girl in Scotland. Herring are traditionally butterflied, pan-fried with an oatmeal coating and served with potatoes. It works equally well with herring fillet.

Rinse the herring fillets and put on a plate. Season with salt and pepper, and brush either side of each fillet with the mustard.

Put the oats in a blender and pulse a few times until partially finely ground; do not overprocess. Put oats in a shallow bowl.

In a medium pan, heat the vegetable oil over medium-high heat.

Press the herring fillets in the oats, coating both sides and shaking off the excess. Put the fillets in the pan skin side up and press down on the fillets with a spatula.

Fry for 2 to 3 minutes until oatmeal is golden brown. Turn and fry another 2 minutes.

MACKEREL

We catch two types of mackerel off Long Island, Spanish mackerel in the summer, and Boston mackerel (also known as Atlantic mackerel) in the winter. Many customers have asked, in all seriousness, if the fish is actually from Spain or Boston. It's locally caught!

There are many types of mackerel, but Boston mackerel is the most common. These are small torpedo-shaped fish, in the tuna family, marked with dark blue wavy lines on their backs. They migrate long distances and swim in large schools. Boston mackerel has oily, dark pink flesh, and a taste comparable to bluefish.

Spanish mackerel are larger and are silver with yellow spots. The flesh is a bit less dark and oily than the Boston mackerel. Many folks who do not like the strong taste of the Boston mackerel love the less-fishy Spanish mackerel.

Their respective seasons are distinct. These fish migrate and are sensitive to water temperature. According to NOAA Fisheries "NOAA scientists have found that environmental factors have changed the distribution patterns of Atlantic mackerel, [...] shifting the stock northeastward and into shallower waters. [...] These findings could have significant implications for U.S. commercial and recreational mackerel fisheries that mostly occur during late winter and early spring." (Northeast Fisheries Science Center, Science Spotlight, August 11, 2011)

Both types of mackerel contain healthy omega-3 fatty acids and are low in mercury, due to the small size of the fish. They can be eaten raw if extremely fresh, and are often smoked or canned.

CRANBERRY-STUFFED MACKEREL

Serves 2

2 Boston mackerel, gutted and headed, with backbone removed (see note)

2 tablespoons chopped sweetened dried cranberries

4 tablespoons panko

2 tablespoons butter, softened, plus 1 tablespoon

2 teaspoons fresh thyme leaves

2 teaspoons Dijon mustard

1 teaspoon salt

This recipe is adapted from one I found in an old Long Island seafood cookbook. The flavors of sweet cranberry, tangy mustard, and oily fish go well together.

Set your oven to 350 degrees.

Clean and rinse the mackerels; remove the backbone and the strip of pin bones on either side. Lay flat on plate and pat dry.

Chop the cranberries and add the panko, 2 tablespoons softened butter, thyme, mustard, and salt. Mix well with a fork or your fingers.

Butter a square of parchment paper with the remaining tablespoon of butter. Lay the mackerels on the parchment paper and stuff each with the cranberry mixture. Use two or three toothpicks to hold the edges of the mackerel together.

Fold the paper around the mackerels until they are enclosed in a parchment package. (Alternatively, you may put the mackerels in a buttered baking dish.)

Bake at 350 degrees for 30 minutes. Unwrap the parchment and carefully remove to a plate. Remove the toothpicks and serve.

Note: To remove the backbone of the gutted and headed mackerel, lay the fish back side down and gently loosen the bones on either side of the backbone. Gently pull the backbone away from the fish. Using kitchen shears, cut the backbone where it meets the tail, leaving the tail on the fish. Remove any pin bones with tweezers.

PAN-FRIED BOSTON MACKEREL WITH COCONUT-GINGER MARINADE

Serves 2

1 pound mackerel fillet

⅓ cup soy sauce

3 tablespoons olive oil

3 tablespoons coconut oil

1 tablespoon packed brown sugar

1 tablespoon grated fresh ginger

2 garlic cloves, minced

2 tablespoons canola oil

The trick to getting a crispy skin on the mackerel is to make sure the fish is dry before putting it in the pan.

Combine all ingredients except for the mackerel and the canola oil; mix well.

Place mackerel in a glass or plastic container with a lid and pour the marinade over the fish. Turn the fish a few times so it is completely coated. Marinate for 30 to 45 minutes under refrigeration.

Remove the mackerel from the marinade and put skin side down on a plate lined with paper towels. Let sit for 8 to 10 minutes.

Turn the fillets skin side up and put back on the plate lined with fresh paper towels. Let sit for 8 to 10 minutes. Pat the skin to make sure it is dry.

Heat 2 tablespoons canola oil in a stainless steel or cast iron pan over medium-high heat (do not use a nonstick pan).

When oil is smoking add the fish, skin side down. When the sides of the fish start to curl press on each fillet with a spatula.

Cook for 3 minutes; do not disturb the fish. After 3 minutes carefully flip the fillets and cook for 1 minute more.

COLD SPICED MACKEREL

Serves 2

1 pound Boston mackerel fillets

3 cups water

½ teaspoon salt

¼ teaspoon allspice

2 bay leaves

1 medium onion, sliced

1 cup grated carrot

½ cup white wine vinegar

3 sprigs fresh parsley

Place mackerel fillets in a saucepan with the water. Add all ingredients and stir; turn heat to medium and cover the pan.

When water begins to bubble turn heat down to medium-low and simmer for 10 minutes, covered.

Turn off the heat, remove the lid and let cool slightly. Remove fish to a container with a lid and cover with the water and vegetables. Refrigerate overnight.

Drain, and serve cold with horseradish or mustard if desired.

BROILED SPANISH MACKEREL WITH MUSTARD SAUCE

Serves 2

1 pound Spanish mackerel
(2 or 3 fillets)

¼ cup olive oil

1 tablespoon Dijon mustard

1 tablespoon white wine vinegar

Salt to taste

2 tablespoons finely chopped
chives (or any other fresh herb;
parsley, basil, tarragon, or
oregano)

Lemon wedges

In a small bowl, stir together the olive oil, mustard, vinegar, and salt.

Set your broiler on high (see note on page 25). Lightly oil a baking sheet or a heavy cast iron or ovenproof skillet. Place the mackerel fillets skin side down.

Brush the fillets liberally with the mustard sauce. Sprinkle with the chives (or other herbs).

Broil without turning for 4 to 6 minutes, until fillets are sizzling. Remove from broiler, squeeze lemon over the fillets, and serve.

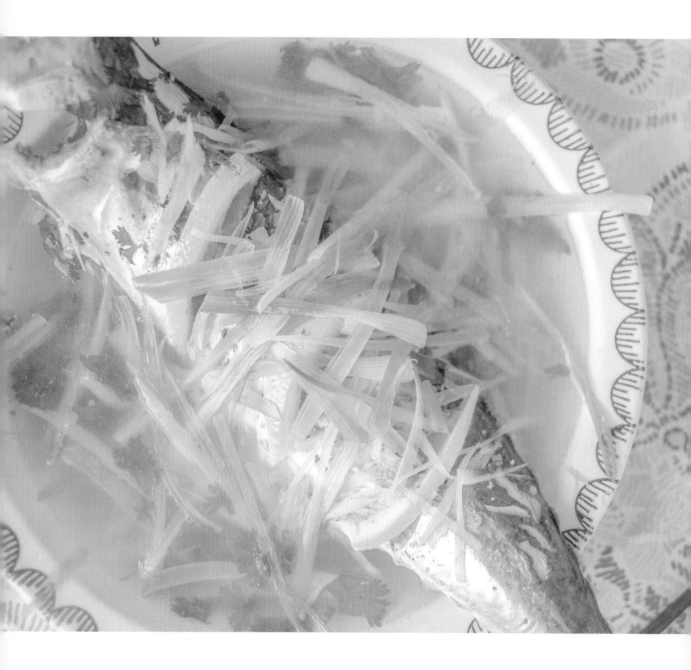

STEAMED WHOLE SPANISH MACKEREL WITH SCALLIONS AND GINGER

Serves 2

1 medium-sized whole Spanish mackerel, gutted, rinsed and dried

1 bunch of scallions

1 4-inch piece of ginger, peeled

½ lemon, sliced into half-moons

2 cups chicken broth

¼ cup dukkah (roasted nuts and spices, pulverized) or roasted sesame seeds

½ cup chopped cilantro

If you do not have a steamer to fit a whole fish, take a deep metal roasting pan and place it over two burners. Inside the roaster place a metal rack or a grid of ramekins to hold a plate with the fish and broth in it. Add a couple of inches of boiling water to the pan. You'll need another pan or a tent of foil to cover the fish while it's steaming.

Trim the scallions of their roots. Cut away the green tops, leaving the lower third of the scallions. Julienne the scallions into long thin pieces. Julienne the ginger into long thin pieces.

Score the fish on either side, then insert the lemon slices into the slits. Put the fish on a plate. Heat the broth to a simmer and put it on the plate beneath the fish.

Cover the fish with the dukkah or sesame seeds, then pile on the ginger and half of the scallions.

Bring the water in your steamer to a low boil, then put the plate with the fish over the water and cover. Steam for 8 minutes, then add the rest of the scallions and steam for another 3 to 5 minutes, until the fish can be easily pulled away from the bone with a fork.

Sprinkle the fish with the cilantro, and serve with the broth. After the fish has been eaten, reserve the broth for a light soup or stock.

SEA TROUT (WEAKFISH)

Sea trout is also known as weakfish, because the weak muscles of the mouth often tear, allowing the fish to escape the fisherman's hook.

These fish are abundant from North Carolina to Massachusetts. They prefer the shallow waters of our local bays and estuaries. We catch them in the spring when they swim north to spawn, and the fall when they head back down south as the water temperature drops.

The local saying on Long Island is that the weakfish start running when the lilacs bloom, around early May. According to an old fish cookbook, you could set your watch by the annual sea trout run; special trains were run from New York City to Greenport for the hordes of fishermen headed east.

We sold a good amount of sea trout in past years, but recently there has not been much around. Regulations were tightened quite a bit in the 1990s, and they remain in place today. Two reasons for the scarcity of sea trout come to mind: temperature rise, which sea trout are sensitive to, and environmental damage to our bays and estuaries. Sea trout depend on eelgrass and the small crustaceans and fish that live there to survive.

Sea trout has a delicate, flaky soft meat, similar to codfish or bluefish. At the fish stand we describe its flavor as between a white fish and a dark fish; more oily and flavorful than flounder, but not as strong as mackerel or blue. It does well baked or broiled; if frying sea trout fillet we recommend rolling it in cornmeal or flour to help hold it together.

BAKED WHOLE SEA TROUT WITH ANCHOVY BUTTER

Serves 2

1 small whole sea trout, scaled and gutted, about 1 ½ to 2 pounds

2 tablespoons unsalted butter

2 tablespoons anchovy butter

2 tablespoons fresh thyme leaves

For Anchovy Butter:

¼ pound softened unsalted butter (one stick)

8 to 10 salted anchovy fillets, rinsed and patted dry

2 teaspoons lemon juice

For the Anchovy Butter:

In blender or food processor, add butter, anchovies, and lemon juice. Process until all ingredients are incorporated.

Heat oven to 400 degrees. Put the unsalted butter in a baking dish large enough to hold the fish. Melt in the hot oven.

Rinse the sea trout and dry thoroughly. When the butter in the baking dish is melted, add the fish. Rub one tablespoon of anchovy butter on the inside cavity of the fish and sprinkle the cavity with one tablespoon of the thyme.

Rub the remaining tablespoon of the anchovy butter on the outside of the fish. Cover with foil and place in the oven.

Bake for 25 to 30 minutes. Use a thin-bladed knife to check down to the bone to see if the fish is cooked all the way through. (It may need another 3 to 5 minutes depending on the size of the fish.)

Sprinkle the remaining tablespoon of thyme over the fish and serve.

TUNA

Out on Long Island, we get several different types of tuna throughout the year. At the fish stand we mostly sell yellowfin and bigeye tuna, along with a small amount of albacore, and some smaller fish like bonito and tunny that are in the tuna family. These types of tuna are plentiful, with the season running roughly from Memorial Day until the end of October or November.

Tuna is considered a highly migratory species, traveling around the globe seasonally. Thus tuna coming into U.S. markets can come from Mexico, South Africa, Hawaii, South America, or anywhere really. Different types of tuna, such as bluefin, yellowfin, bigeye, skipjack, albacore, or blackfin, have different levels of sustainability and are regulated by five different world bodies.

When people order tuna they are typically thinking of yellowfin, a glowing, ruby red steak. Bigeye steaks, comparable in quality to the yellowfin, have a looser, less firm texture. Albacore, which hits in the summer, has a lighter-tasting meat that is less flavorful than other types of tuna. It is generally less expensive but can still be eaten raw and has a distinct taste.

There is also skipjack tuna around in late September; it is a dark-fleshed version of the fish, almost like a cross between a tuna and a mackerel. At that same time of year the bonitos show up, with dark reddish-brown flesh, a favorite among our Japanese customers. We get little tunnys as well: portly little silver torpedoes with dark blue hash marks down their backs —perfect to throw on the barbecue grill.

The most coveted type of tuna is bluefin, which we do not sell. Quite a bit of bluefin is caught here off Long Island, and most of it is sold directly to Japan. Japanese buyers come out to the docks in Montauk and Shinnecock and take a core sample of the meat with a thin, hollow tube, almost like a needle, to assess quality. One fish can go for tens of thousands of dollars. This summer Alex's friend caught a bluefin tuna weighing over five hundred pounds. He had a special commercial license to take it, sold it to a Japanese buyer, and took his year out of the red with one fish.

Unfortunately, the National Marine Fisheries Service has not closed the bluefin tuna fishery, especially since one of their spawning grounds is the Gulf of Mexico, which was decimated by the BP oil spill. Bluefin are severely overfished. However, Alex told me that this past year has been a good one for bluefin around Long Island and there have been lots of fish around (that happens a lot —the fishermen report something different than what the prevailing notion is); so much so that the Department of Environmental Conservation actually raised the quota. Personally I think bluefin tuna should be closed until the stocks are rebuilt, so I make a choice not to eat it. Our local seasonal tunas more than satisfy.

Outside of the season I rarely eat fresh tuna, but I am a big fan of canned, oil-packed tuna, especially those from Italy or Spain. Tuna is high in omega-3 fatty acids and the health benefits are so great that I continue to eat it in the off-season (plus, it's delicious and easy to prepare). An eight-ounce portion once every week is fine; any more than that and you run the risk of elevating your mercury level, as Alex found out. He had been eating canned yellowfin tuna on the boat every day while he towed his net waiting for it to fill up with fish. Sure enough, his mercury level was elevated, and the doctor immediately quizzed him about his diet. After laying off the canned tuna for a few weeks he was back to normal. Eating tuna every day is not a good idea!

Cooking tuna

The most important rule when cooking tuna (and all fish, really) is not to overcook it. The first time I ever made a tuna steak I cooked it way too long. It was white and hard as a rock and it ended up tasting like shoe leather. I threw it out and sulked over my dinner of plain white rice. It was a lesson I never forgot.

Most of the time, the tuna we sell is suitable to eat raw, so we like to sear the outside of the steak and leave the inside rare. Start out with a hot pan and a few tablespoons of oil (I use olive or grapeseed oil, which has a high smoking point), then drop the steak in and let it cook for two minutes per side. Take it out of the pan and cut into the center of it. If the tuna is too rare for you, put it back in the pan and cook another minute or two per side. It won't need much more time than that.

Once you sear a steak once or twice you can get a feel for how long the cooking time is to prepare the fish to your liking. Err on the side of undercooking —you can always put the fish back on the grill or the pan for a few more minutes.

Tuna is often marinated to give it some flavor. Generally speaking, don't marinate fish for more than 45 minutes or so; there is no need to marinate for hours as with beef or chicken. Put the tuna and the marinade in a shallow Tupperware container with a lid, or just a shallow dish covered with plastic wrap, or even a ziplock bag, and refrigerate it. Once or twice during the 45 minute period turn the fish so the marinade can penetrate the fish equally. Sometimes I marinate less if I am short on time, but you need at least 20 minutes of marination time.

Marinating any kind of fish with a very acidic marinade can actually cook the fish (see Scallop Ceviche recipe, on page 162). To prevent this, use only a small amount of vinegar or citrus juice in your marinade.

Can I eat it raw?

If you want to serve fish raw, make sure you look closely at it and give it the smell test before you buy it. It should look fresh, firm, and glowing. I start recommending the tuna for fish of the day at the stand when I see that every piece is glowing deep red. Fresh tuna looks like a tub of beautiful jewels, but if it looks soft or the color is off it doesn't necessarily mean that it is not fresh. For example, bigeye tuna is naturally a little looser in texture and darker in color. Ask your fishmonger what type of tuna they are offering, and try to become familiar with what the different types should look and feel like. I have seen customers pass up exceedingly fresh albacore tuna because it "didn't look red enough." What a mistake! If the tuna looks off or smells bad in any way, either cook it or choose another type of fish.

FDA guidelines call for any fish that is to be eaten raw to be frozen first, except for tuna and shellfish. Most of the tuna used at Japanese restaurants has been flash frozen; that is, frozen at a very cold temperature so that any parasites or pathogens have been killed. It is up to the consumer to educate themselves on the issue and decide whether to eat raw fish or not. If your immune system is compromised in any way it is not advisable to eat raw fish.

Fun fact

Some tuna sold in neighborhood delis and supermarkets is treated with carbon monoxide. Yes, you read that right . . . the stuff that comes out of your car exhaust. They use this method on old tuna so that it turns cherry red and looks fresh. It is difficult to spot the difference, even for me, and I have handled tuna for over twenty years. So how can you tell? If you see sushi made with bright, unnaturally glowing red tuna and it is sold at a cheap price, then that tuna has been treated. Think about it: if the tuna really was such high-quality it would not be sold in delis and supermarkets at such a low price.

TUNA TARTARE

Serves 2

1 ¼ pounds tuna, any thickness, trimmed of bloodline and fat

4 scallions, chopped (use white and green parts)

3 tablespoons ponzu sauce

1 tablespoon sesame oil

2 teaspoons grated ginger

¼ teaspoon prepared wasabi paste

½ lemon, juiced (about 2 tablespoons)

Salt to taste

Olive oil

With a sharp knife cut the tuna into 1/8 inch dice. In a large bowl combine the tuna with the scallions, ponzu, sesame oil, ginger, wasabi and lemon juice. Mix gently, then season with salt to your liking.

Serve the tartare in the center of a salad plate, forming it into a small mound by hand or with a mold. Finish by drizzling a good olive oil on top.

ALEX'S MARINATED TUNA

Serves 4

For the Marinade:

½ cup soy sauce

1 tablespoon grated ginger

1 tablespoon sesame oil

1 tablespoon lemon juice

½ tablespoon minced garlic

1 teaspoon sriracha sauce (optional)

4 tuna steaks, ¾ to 1 inch thick, about 8 ounces each

4 tablespoons prepared wasabi

My dad still talks about Alex's marinated tuna, which we laid out on an enormous grill borrowed from the Methodist Church's annual chicken barbecue. It was Alex's 50th birthday party and our guests raved about the flavor of this salty and spicy marinade. It was such a big hit that it's now one of our go-to recipes for parties of all sizes. Prepared wasabi —a blend of wasabi powder, horseradish and mustard, generally sold in grocery stores that stock Asian items— is served on the side.

For the Marinade:

Put all ingredients in a blender; process until combined.

Put the tuna steaks in a shallow dish, plastic container or resealable plastic bag, and pour the marinade over them. Cover and refrigerate for 45 minutes. Turn the steaks occasionally during that time so they can absorb the marinade evenly.

Light a cleaned and oiled grill. Grill the steaks over high heat until cooked on the outside, about 2 to 3 minutes. Turn and grill for another 2 to 3 minutes, checking one of the steaks with a thin-bladed knife to see if it is cooked to your liking. If you like your tuna well-done, continue cooking for another 2 minutes per side.

Use the same procedure for a stovetop grill pan using medium-high heat.

Serve each steak with 1 tablespoon of the prepared wasabi on the side.

TUNA KABOBS

Serves 4

1 ½ to 2 pounds tuna chunks, trimmed of bloodline and fat

1 medium onion, peeled, halved, and cut into wedges

1 red bell pepper, stemmed, seeded and cut into 1-inch strips

1 portobello mushroom, cut into 8 triangular slices

2 tomatoes, halved and cut into wedges (or 12 cherry tomatoes left whole)

For the Marinade:

2 cloves garlic, peeled and minced

3 tablespoons Dijon mustard

2 tablespoons olive oil

1 tablespoon sesame oil

2 teaspoons lemon juice

1 teaspoon salt

1 teaspoon sugar

¾ teaspoon pepper

After a day at the market we often end up with a bag full of what we call "tuna chunks," which are just the ends of the tuna loin. The meat is the same quality, but the pieces are irregularly shaped and often have a bloodline and fatty striations running through them. Sliced, they sauté quickly and are perfect over rice or pasta. Other times we use them for a really fresh-tasting tuna salad or even grind them up into patties to make tuna burgers.

Tuna chunks are also excellent for kabobs. You will need a set of metal or wooden skewers for this recipe. Serve them as is, or over noodles or rice.

For the Marinade:

In a small bowl, whisk all ingredients together.

Put the tuna chunks in a shallow dish, plastic container, or resealable plastic bag and pour the marinade over them. Cover and refrigerate for 45 minutes.

After marinating, skewer the tuna chunks and vegetables, alternating in whatever way you like.

Light a cleaned and oiled grill. Grill the kabobs on a hot fire for about 4 minutes per side. If you like you can broil the kabobs in the oven turning them after about 3 minutes on each side to brown all sides.

Kabobs can be served over rice or noodles, or as is.

STUFFED TUNA STEAKS

Serves 4

2 pounds tuna steaks, ¾ to 1 inch thick, trimmed of bloodline and fat

For the Marinade:

3 tablespoons olive oil

1 tablespoon sesame oil

1 tablespoon fresh lemon thyme leaves

1 garlic clove, minced

For the Stuffing:

12 green manzanilla olives, pitted and chopped

2 tablespoons diced red onion

1 tablespoon chopped fresh parsley

1 garlic clove, minced

1 tablespoon olive oil

½ teaspoon grated lemon peel

¼ teaspoon salt

¼ teaspoon freshly ground black pepper

This dish is based on a Mark Bittman recipe from his excellent book Fish. *It is a very elegant recipe that guests love and appears much more difficult than it really is. Make a horizontal slice in the edge of the tuna steak, enlarging a pocket in the center while being careful not to cut through the other edge of the steak. You can stuff it with whatever filling you like.*

To make the marinade, combine all ingredients and marinate the tuna steaks in a shallow dish or plastic container in the refrigerator while you make the stuffing. Tuna should be marinated for 20 to 45 minutes.

To make the stuffing, combine all ingredients and mix well.

Remove tuna from marinade and dry on paper towels. Using a small sharp knife, make a horizontal slice through the side of the tuna steak, creating a pocket. Be sure not to cut all the way through the other side of the steak.

Fill each pocket with the stuffing. Insert a toothpick or two through the edges of the pocket opening to hold it closed.

Grill or pan sear the tuna, about 3 or 4 minutes on each side for a 1-inch thick steak.

TUNA CRUDO WITH OLIVES, ANCHOVIES, AND CUCUMBER SALAD

**Serves 2 as a Main dish or
4 as an Appetizer**

For the Cucumber Salad:

1 medium cucumber, peeled, seeded, halved lengthwise and sliced about ¼ inch thick

1 tablespoon salt

2 tablespoons olive oil

Lemon wedge

Salt and pepper to taste

For the Crudo:

¾ to 1 pound tuna, ¾ to 1 inch thick, suitable to eat raw

½ of a lemon, juiced (about 2 tablespoons)

⅓ cup black olives, pitted and chopped

1 tin (2 ounces) anchovies, rinsed and chopped

1 tablespoon capers, rinsed and drained

2 tablespoons olive oil

Sea salt

Recipe by Gerard Mossé

"Crudo" is the Italian word for "raw." This makes a simple, light appetizer or dinner with a crisp cucumber salad accompaniment. When salting the cucumbers, weigh them down with something (we use a container of milk on a plate or a ziplock bag full of ice) to help force more moisture out of them and prevent them from getting soggy in the process. Be sure to make the cucumber salad at least one hour in advance so the cucumbers have time to drain.

For the Cucumber Salad:

Toss the cucumber and salt in a colander. Set the colander in a large bowl and place in the refrigerator to drain for one hour. Rinse and pat dry.

In a medium bowl, whisk together the olive oil, a squeeze of lemon and salt and pepper. Add cucumbers; toss to coat.

For the Crudo:

Slice tuna into approximately ¼ inch thick slices. For an appetizer, use about two ounces per person (3 or 4 slices). For a main dish, use 6 to 8 ounces per person (9 or 10 slices).

Spoon a tablespoon of lemon juice onto each of two plates. Fan out the tuna slices on top of the lemon juice.

In a small bowl add the olives, anchovies and capers. Mix together with one tablespoon of olive oil. Put one tablespoon of this mixture on either side of the tuna slices. Drizzle the tuna with the remaining tablespoon of olive oil, sprinkle with sea salt and serve with the cucumber salad.

STEPH'S TUNA SALAD

Serves 4

1 ½ to 2 pounds cooked tuna steaks or chunks

½ cup mayonnaise

1 tablespoon sesame oil

2 or 3 scallions, chopped (use both white and green parts)

⅓ to ½ cup diced carrots

⅓ cup chopped green olives

¼ cup chopped fresh parsley

Salt and pepper to taste

1 teaspoon olive oil (optional)

I use leftover grilled tuna to make this salad, but you can also poach the tuna and then cool it before using.

In a large bowl, break up the tuna with your fingers into small bite-sized pieces.

Mix the mayonnaise, sesame oil, scallions, carrots, olives, and parsley with the tuna. Combine well. Add salt and pepper to taste. If you feel the tuna is too dry add a little bit of olive oil.

Serve on a bed of lettuce or make a sandwich using a wrap, a crusty baguette, or whole wheat bread.

POACHED TUNA PACKED IN OIL

Serves 4

1 ½ to 2 pounds tuna steaks or chunks, trimmed of bloodline and fat

4 to 6 cups cold water

½ a medium orange, sliced into rounds (or 1 lemon, seeded and sliced into rounds)

10 peppercorns

5 sprigs fresh parsley

2 bay leaves

Olive oil

I have a few customers who buy a lot of tuna while it is in season, poach it and pack it in oil. It keeps this way for one week in the refrigerator, so there is tuna on hand whenever they like.

Put the water in a large dutch oven or a deep saucepan and add the tuna. Add the orange (or lemon), peppercorns, parsley, and bay leaves, making sure the fish is covered by at least ½ inch of liquid.

Cover the saucepan and poach tuna over low heat until cooked through, about 10 to 15 minutes. Let cool.

Pack tuna into a glass jar and cover with olive oil. Store in the refrigerator for up to 1 week.

LOST AT SEA

A friend of Alex's named Tovey steamed out of Mattituck Inlet early one October morning to pull his lobster pots just like all the other lobstermen. Later that same day at dusk, a man walking on a beach in Fairfield, Connecticut, across the Sound from Mattituck, found Tovey's empty boat beached, the throttle pushed down, the engine still running, and no one around.

This was back in the early 90s when there were plenty of lobster in the Sound, and thus plenty of lobstermen. A lobsterman's job was routine: setting and pulling around six or eight hundred traps, called pots. Each one was a simple wire cage baited with a "trash fish," like bunker or herring, and weighted with a twenty pound brick. Baited, the big wire cages were dropped overboard with a sixty foot line attached, and each had a colored buoy floating above that indicated the lobsterman's colors and permit number. After each trap was set, the lobsterman marked latitude and longitude on a plotter, then let out the line and moved on to the next location. They did this all day: a single line might have three to five hundred pots on it.

Tovey and his friends Jethro and Gary ran their own boats. Alex and I lived in a little cottage on a hill overlooking Mattituck Inlet, and I would hear the boats coming back in the late afternoon, each engine sounding a little different: Tovey's a low burr, Jethro's a little whine, and Gary announcing his return by unfailingly blasting rock and roll. Later, I would hear Alex's boat chugging towards the dock, and involuntarily breathe a sigh of relief. There was something about the listening that I remember most. I found myself listening every day around the time when Alex was supposed to be back. I'd hear it first, then look out the window to see the *Blue Moon* moving toward me on a thin strip of dark blue water. After a while I didn't have to look for it anymore, just listen. I knew when each of these guys had come in. Then one day I didn't hear Tovey.

Most everyone thought his foot had gotten tangled in the trawl line, the looped line that speeds over the side of the boat after the weighted pot is dropped. He was probably pulled overboard. All lobstermen carry a knife on their belt in case they need to cut that line quickly, but I guess Tovey didn't have time.

I didn't know him very well; I had met him just once at a party at Alex's house: he was a tanned, gangly guy with sandy hair, and he laughed all night long. Tovey grew up in Mattituck with a tight group of friends, and all became fishermen. Tovey and his friend Gary, the wildest of the four, used to take their boats to school every day, tie them up at the town dock at the end of Love Lane and cross the road to

Mattituck High School. When these guys weren't working on the water, they were playing on the water on their days off. They stayed out late and started work late too, because, as Gary said, "The lobsters aren't going anywhere."

Tovey's mother called the Coast Guard when he didn't return home that night. The Sound was searched with boats and a plane. All the fishermen were out looking for him, and continued to make trips even after the search was officially called off. For a while Alex was anxious he might pull Tovey's body up in his net. Some of the guys started wearing safety harnesses, but that didn't last long. Too hot, too uncomfortable, and too likely to get tangled in the wires. Old habits reasserted themselves, and things went on as they always had, only with Tovey missing.

Over the years I became friends with Tovey's girlfriend Mercy. She was a member of the small circle of fishing families; we were about the same age and lived across the inlet from one another. Occasionally she would mention him, likening him to a young John Kennedy. Tovey's family was wealthy and sailing was in their blood. I was over at Mercy's one day when a New York television station called to interview her about his disappearance. "Fuck off!" she said, and slammed down the phone.

Tovey's mother spent years raising money to create a Lost at Sea memorial. Eventually, a colossal sculpture of a fisherman standing in a dory, pulling in his net, was raised next to the big brown and white lighthouse at Montauk Point. The dedication of the memorial took place on a dreary gray fall day in a light drizzle. Everyone was muted and wet. I showed up, carrying a bunch of damp flowers from the farmers' market, and was surprised to see Billy Joel there too, looking particularly sad-eyed. He had hung out with Tovey over at the Old Mill in Mattituck on one of his trips to the North Fork, back when the fishermen used to go there, before it got too fancy.

The Lost at Sea memorial includes the names of men carved into its pink granite base. The first ones are dated 1719, and you can run your finger down the list and see the groups of seamen that went down together. 1866 was a bad year, there are twenty-three names listed, with no mention of what happened or if they went down together on one vessel or not. I recognized many of the names as the local families that settled the area, but just as many were from away.

Tovey went missing in 1994; the last name on the list is dated 1998. There have been lots of fatal accidents and close calls since then, but being lost is a special kind of hell for those left behind.

CLAMS

Long Island is famous for the quality and quantity of its clams found in the Sound and in the many protected bays and inlets of the Island. Native Americans first showed settlers their harvesting techniques in the 1600s, and the commercial clamming industry began in the 1830s. Today there are many baymen raising clams and oysters with aquaculture ventures throughout the Island, in addition to harvesting wild sets of clams. Alex spent quite a few winters in the Great South Bay harvesting wild clams using a chainsaw to cut through the ice.

Clams are available year-round and harvesting is strictly regulated by the New York State Department of Environmental Conservation. In an effort to improve food safety procedures, the DEC's Shellfishing Section recently strengthened regulations for harvesters and dealers with respect to temperature control and tagging. Each bushel of shellfish is immediately tagged with the harvester's name, shellfish digger's permit number, harvest location, amount, time and date. Whoever buys the clams is required to check for the tag. A harvester, fish store, or restaurant in possession of untagged shellfish is subject to a big fine.

Periodically the NYDEC will close certain areas to shellfishing, especially after a big rain which can send contaminated runoff into the water. The harvest areas are strictly monitored by the DEC and the local townships for water quality that can make the shellfish unfit to eat. There is a hotline harvesters can call to check on particular areas; they also are notified by mail.

Here are some clam varieties native to Long Island:

Hard-shell Clams (also called quahogs): From smallest to largest: they include littlenecks, topnecks, cherrystones, and chowder clams. Eat these raw on the half shell, or steam them open and serve with melted butter. Hard-shells can be baked, fried, or made into chowder or stews.

Soft-shell Clams (also called steamers or piss clams): These have a more delicate shell that is not tightly closed; usually the neck of the clam sticks out and occasionally will squirt you. These should be cooked and are most often steamed or fried.

Razor Clams: These are long, thin clams that look like an old-fashioned straight razor. The clam inside is thick and meaty. My Spanish and Chinese customers in particular really love these clams; they throw them on the grill as is or cook them with black bean sauce. We usually sell them in the spring and the fall but they are not easy to get; in the past few years the season has been closed except for the dead of winter.

Skimmer Clams (also called surf clams): These are large clams found in the Sound or offshore. The minimum size you can keep is 3 inches; they can grow up to 8 inches long. These are commercially harvested and sold processed. Alex first came to the North Fork when he was clamming for skimmers right off of Mattituck Inlet in the early '90s; tractor trailer loads of Mattituck skimmers were sold to Campbell's for their clam chowder.

Choose clam sizes based on the type of dish you are making. For eating raw on the half shell, choose small to medium clams (littlenecks to topnecks). For stuffing and baking, use cherrystones or chowder clams. For chowders or stews you may use any size clams, but the larger ones contain more meat and juice. Make sure to use a generous amount of clams for your chowder or clam pie so you can really taste the briny flavor.

How to store clams

It's best to take the clams out of the plastic bag you buy them in and immediately put them in a bowl or a colander set over a bowl. Put them uncovered in the refrigerator; preferably at the bottom shelf in the back where it's coldest. You may lay a damp paper towel on top of the bowl if you like; as long as they are cold and can breathe they will last quite a while in the fridge, 4 or 5 days for hard-shells and 1 to 2 days for soft-shells.

Don't let the clams sit in water (they will die if not in salt water). To soak the clams in order to clean out any sand, put them in a big pot or bowl filled with salt water (a half-cup of salt added to a big pot of water is fine). If you like, add a half-cup of cornmeal to the water. This irritates the clam, causing it to spit out the grit inside it. You can leave the pot in the fridge for a couple of hours if you have time. When ready to use them, take them out of the pot and rinse them with cold running water.

If you open a clam and it is full of mud or it has a bad smell, discard it. If you are cooking clams and all the clams open except for one, discard it. Eating bad clams can make you very sick, so if in doubt, do not eat!

ALEX'S MANHATTAN CLAM CHOWDER

Serves 8

5 dozen large clams, opened and chopped in bite-size pieces, with their juice

6 pieces bacon, chopped

2 medium onions, diced

6 medium carrots, peeled and cut into rounds

6 medium potatoes (Yukon Gold or white), skin on, cut in 1-inch chunks

4 large celery stalks, with leaves, chopped

32 ounces canned whole plum tomatoes

1 pound frozen corn kernels

2 ½ teaspoons Old Bay seasoning

2 teaspoons chopped fresh oregano (or ½ teaspoon dried)

½ tablespoon black pepper

5 bay leaves

1 to 1 ½ quarts clam juice or fish stock, or a combination (be sure to strain clam juice from the just-opened clams)

This is a Manhattan clam chowder recipe by an honest-to-goodness Manhattanite. Alex has made this so many times he knows the recipe by heart. In the fall and winter he makes an enormous pot and puts a couple of quarts in the freezer.

In large stockpot sauté bacon and onions over medium-low heat until soft. Add all ingredients except chopped clams to pot. Bring to a boil; turn heat to low and simmer uncovered for 45 minutes.

Add clams and cook for another 5 to 8 minutes.

LIGHT NEW ENGLAND STYLE CHOWDER

Serves 6

36 cherrystone clams, rinsed

2 cups water

¼ pound bacon, diced

1 cup chopped white onion

1 cup chopped celery, about
2 stalks

¼ cup chopped celery leaves

3 bay leaves

Pepper to taste

3 large potatoes (Yukon Gold
or white), peeled and chopped
into small cubes

1 cup heavy cream

2 tablespoons butter

¼ cup chopped fresh parsley

As Emeril Lagasse says in one of his cookbooks, there are as many ways to make clam chowder as there are to make gumbo in New Orleans. It depends on where you are from. The recipes are very different state to state.

My dad's family is from Boston, and we lived for a while in Fall River, Massachusetts. My mother sent me a sheaf of recipes for chowders from all over New England, from Mystic to Boston to Rhode Island to Maine, and these range from very creamy to just a little cream, and from fairly spicy to not spicy at all.

Classic New England chowder contains only a few ingredients: onions sautéed with bacon or salt pork, fresh clams with their juice, potatoes, and milk or heavy cream. Adjust the ingredients to your liking, and make sure to buy enough clams. I am convinced that one reason our homemade clam chowders are so good is because we use at least three dozen clams, sometimes more. In many restaurant chowders you can't even taste the clams, and what's the point of that?

This chowder is fairly thin and not too creamy; you can taste the clams and vegetables —I especially like the celery flavor.

Add clams and 2 cups water to large pot; cover and steam over medium-high heat until clams open, about 4 to 5 minutes. Take pot off the heat and cool, reserving the liquid in the pot.

Remove clams from shells over a bowl, collecting any liquid from the shells. Chop clams; strain clam liquid and reserve (you should have about 3 cups).

Over medium-low heat, sauté bacon in large pot, about 3 to 4 minutes. When partially cooked, add onion, celery, celery leaves and bay leaves. Season with pepper and sauté until soft, about 5 minutes.

Add strained clam juice, potatoes, heavy cream, and butter. Simmer for 15 minutes.

Add chopped clams and parsley. Stir well. Remove bay leaves and serve.

CAJUN STUFFED CLAMS

Serves 2 to 4

2 dozen large clams (littlenecks or cherrystones)

1 stick unsalted butter

4 tablespoons olive oil

2 cups chopped onion

1 ½ cups chopped bell pepper

1 cup finely chopped celery

1 heaping tablespoon minced garlic

2 bay leaves

1 cup water

1 cup bread crumbs

Parsley or chives, chopped, for optional garnish

For Spice Mix:

1 teaspoon salt

½ teaspoon cayenne pepper

½ teaspoon black pepper

¼ teaspoon onion powder

¼ teaspoon dried thyme leaves

Large pinch white pepper

Large pinch dried oregano

This is a spicy take on the typical baked clam recipe. My peeves with baked clams are too much breading and cheese (I am one of those purists who find cheese on any type of seafood abhorrent. Add it if you must!).

Combine the spice mix ingredients and set aside.

Heat the butter and the olive oil in a large skillet. Add half of the vegetables and sauté over medium heat for 15 minutes, stirring often.

Add the rest of the vegetables, garlic and bay leaves, and continue cooking for 10 minutes, stirring often.

Add one cup of water and the spice mix to the pan. Bring to a boil and simmer for 5 minutes.

Remove from heat and discard bay leaves. Add ¾ cup of the bread crumbs and mix.

Rinse the clams and add them to a large pot containing 1½ cups of simmering water. Cover and steam over low heat until the clams open, about 4 to 5 minutes. Remove the clams to a large bowl; strain and reserve liquid.

Remove clams from shells and chop finely. Separate the shell halves and reserve.

Add 2 cups of the strained clam liquid to the stuffing mixture in the pan. Bring to a simmer and continue cooking until mixture thickens. Add chopped clams and stir; remove from heat.

Arrange the clam shells on a large baking sheet. Spoon the stuffing into the clam shells, sprinkling each with the remaining bread crumbs.

Broil under high heat until sizzling and browned on top (see note on page 25).

If desired, sprinkle chopped parsley or chives over clams. Serve with lemon slices.

SPAGHETTI WITH CLAM SAUCE

Serves 4

4 dozen littleneck clams, rinsed

1 pound spaghetti

1 tablespoon olive oil

¼ pound bacon, diced

1 small white onion, diced

5 cloves garlic, crushed and roughly chopped

1 teaspoon hot pepper flakes

1 bunch fresh parsley, chopped

This is our go-to one-pot pasta and clam dish. We like it with bacon and tons of parsley; feel free to add or subtract ingredients as you wish. Use one dozen clams per person.

Bring a large pot of salted water to a boil. Cook the spaghetti according to the package directions and drain.

In a large pot with a tight-fitting lid, heat the olive oil over medium heat. Add the bacon and cook for about 3 to 4 minutes. Add the onion, garlic and hot pepper flakes and continue to cook for another 3 to 4 minutes until onion and garlic are softened.

Add the clams to the pot and stir well with the other ingredients. Put the lid on the pot and steam for 4 to 5 minutes until the clams open.

Add the chopped parsley, stir well, and turn off the heat.

Put the spaghetti in a large serving bowl and pour the contents of the pot over the pasta. Serve in individual pasta bowls.

LARRY'S CLAMS CASINO

Serves 2 to 4

2 dozen littleneck clams, small sizes

¼ cup finely chopped green bell pepper

¼ cup minced garlic

4 to 6 strips of bacon

Recipe by Larry Racies

Larry was one of our all-time favorite customers at the fish stand. He was in his 80s when he (and his wife, Gail) first started buying clams from us —two dozen every week— and he was the only customer we let choose the clams himself. Larry was a very positive, ebullient guy, greeting everyone by name in a loud cheery voice. He was a cameraman at CBS back in the day and told lots of stories about the old days and personalities like Richard Nixon, Dan Rather, and Weegee (photographer Arthur Fellig). He drove a giant Cadillac with his press pass still on the dashboard. Larry, you are missed!

Set broiler to high (see note on page 25).

Shuck the clams, separating the shell halves. Leave each clam in one half of the shell; discard the other shell.

Place the half shells on a baking sheet. You may place them on a bed of rock salt or a crumpled piece of aluminum foil to prevent them from tipping if you like.

Fill each shell half with equal amounts of the pepper and the garlic.

Cut the bacon strips into pieces large enough to cover a shell completely and place a piece over each shell half.

Broil the clams until the bacon is cooked, approximately 5 minutes. Do not overcook. Serve immediately.

CLAMS AND PORK FRICASSEE

Serves 4

1 pound boneless pork

2 dozen topneck clams, shucked

For the Marinade:

1 cup dry white wine

3 teaspoons paprika

3 bay leaves

4 whole cloves

6 cloves garlic, chopped

6 tablespoons olive oil

1 cup chopped onions

1 ½ cups tomatoes (peeled, seeded and diced)

Salt and pepper to taste

3 tablespoons chopped fresh cilantro

3 tablespoons chopped fresh parsley

Recipe by Chef Ed Sun, Sun Culinary Arts

The day before preparing the meal, place pork in a glass or porcelain bowl. Make the marinade by mixing the wine, paprika, bay leaves, cloves, and half of the chopped garlic. Pour over pork and refrigerate overnight.

The next day drain the pork in a colander, saving the marinade. Pat the meat dry. Open the clams (if they are difficult to open you may steam them), retain juice.

In a large frying pan, heat 2 tablespoons of the olive oil over medium heat; add the onions, tomatoes and the rest of the chopped garlic. Cook until softened.

In another frying pan, heat 3 tablespoons of olive oil over high heat. Add the pork. Cook until all sides are browned, flipping the meat occasionally.

Add the pork and the marinade to the pan with the vegetables. Cook for 20 minutes (add extra clam juice if needed). Add the clams and cook briefly, do not overcook.

Remove from heat to a platter, pouring the vegetables and clams over the pork. Season with salt and pepper (keep in mind the clams are salty so do not oversalt). Mix the cilantro and parsley together and sprinkle over the dish.

LOBSTER
(THE END OF LONG ISLAND LOBSTER AS WE ONCE KNEW IT)

When I first moved out to Mattituck, eating lobster was a common thing. There was so much of it around any time you wanted it, I thought I had died and gone to heaven. Big platters piled with bright red lobsters and giant bowls of lobster salad at parties. I made glowing orange pots of lobster bisque with lots of cream and butter. Lobster was so bountiful that Alex used to trade them for baloney sandwiches at the deli, if you can imagine. Times were good for quite a while, but one summer it all changed.

We sold lobsters at the fish stand for years until the big die-off. Until then there were lots of little lobsters in the Long Island Sound, about 1 to 3 pounds on average, or what people called "chickens." Offshore in the ocean there was a separate lobster fishery, where Alex worked years ago, pulling sixty pots on a trawl. There were several very good boom years; all of the lobstermen were driving around in enormous new pickup trucks. They all worked every day and were flush with cash and red in the cheeks with happiness. Some of them even set up roadside lobster stands and made even more money from the summer people.

Then in 1999, the West Nile virus was discovered in the area. Mosquitoes carry the virus and transmit it when they bite a human or an animal. Local officials took action and decided to spray malathion and other pesticides in the estuaries and the marshy areas where the mosquitoes bred.

There were a few deaths from West Nile, usually elderly people, and folks were getting nervous about a possible epidemic. So in the end they decided not just to spray out East, but all 1400 square miles of Long Island.

And the spraying wasn't limited to Long Island —I remember being at a backyard barbecue in Brooklyn and seeing a low-flying plane pass overhead, spraying chemicals. One of the fishermen complained about the toxic stuff they were spraying —it supposedly wasn't harmful to people or animals. "They make an announcement before they spray and tell people to close their windows and keep pregnant women and small children inside." This fisherman had a young daughter, and he was suspicious about the chemical wash raining from the sky. "Why make an announcement to close the windows and stay inside if the stuff they're spraying is safe?"

Malathion is an insecticide that is commonly used to kill mosquitoes, and unfortunately lobsters are closely related to insects. Scientists from Stony Brook University, under the Long Island Sound Lobster Research Initiative, pinpointed the four days that 50% of the lobster population died. On September 19, a coastal storm "dumped heavy rain on Long Island and flushed pesticides into the Sound in storm runoff." That, coupled with several weeks of high water temperatures, caused a major die-off from September 19th to the 22nd. And that was the end of the one hundred million dollar lobster industry in New York and Connecticut.

We knew quite a few fishermen who were affected by the die-off. They lost their livelihoods, and for some of them it took a mental toll. They would still go out every day pulling their pots, only to find limp, dead lobsters. Any that were still alive usually didn't make it very long. Some of the lobstermen turned to fishing or conching (catching a local type of sea snail worth very little). Some of the lobstermen quit altogether, taking "straight" jobs at Home Depot or elsewhere, or they relied on side jobs, like running a charter boat or working on marine engines, but it wasn't easy. A few started drinking. For others it took years for them to admit that lobstering was over, and we might never see them in the numbers that we had in the past. Long Island Sound is the southernmost reach of the lobster habitat, and with warming waters the fishery might never be reestablished in the Sound.

It was never proven conclusively that the malathion caused the die-off, but the makers of the pesticide settled with the lobstermen in a class action lawsuit for twelve and a half million dollars.

And that's why we don't sell lobster at the fish stand anymore. I actually thought that someday the population might come back, but it hasn't so far. According to the Connecticut Department of Energy and Environmental Protection, "Lobster landings in Long Island Sound have declined from 3.7 million pounds in 1998 to just 142,000 pounds in 2011. Between 1984 and 1998 state lobster landings averaged 2.3 million pounds. Lobster abundance and landings in the Sound have declined steadily, and are at record low levels at this time. The central and western Sound, where landings have fallen by 99% since 1998, has seen the greatest decline in lobster abundance."

There are a few lobsters around, but not nearly enough to make them worth fishing for. The ones I've seen aren't healthy; they're weak and die quickly. The combination of warming waters and the pollution flowing into the Long Island Sound from the rivers in Connecticut and the pesticide-laden lawns of homeowners have made it difficult for the lobsters to reestablish themselves. People still come out here looking for a lobster dinner, but the lobsters aren't local anymore.

Most of the lobster caught in the Northeast comes from either Maine or Canada. Both places have had record landings the past few years; Maine landed more than 123 million pounds in 2012, up 18 million pounds from the year before. There is so much lobster in Maine that the lobstermen are finding it a challenge to find markets for it all.

Florida lobster (Spiny lobster)

Florida lobster are clawless, with two sets of antennae covered with spines. They tend to have a harder shell and a more dense meat than the northern clawed lobster. They are abundant in the shallow, warm waters of the Keys, and both commercial and recreational fisheries there are heavily regulated.

You will find the spiny lobster in local seafood markets, but they are not cheap. Keys prices run $25 to $30 per tail, and $12 to $18 per whole lobster.

We have a commercial fisherman friend in the Keys who has been fishing for spiny lobster for years, through hurricanes and the oil spill. He reports that for the last few years, the market has been dominated by the Chinese, who have been buying up the supply at more than decent prices (but also driving up the prices for the locals).

LOBSTER ROLL

Serves 4

3 pounds cooked lobster meat (about four 1 ¼ to 1 ½ pound lobsters), chopped into half-inch pieces

4 tablespoons mayonnaise

2 stalks celery, finely chopped

2 teaspoons lemon juice

2 teaspoons chopped fresh dill

Salt and pepper to taste

4 hot dog buns, top split (use the regular kind if you can't find top split buns)

4 tablespoons butter, softened

Lemon wedges

Imagine my surprise and delight when a local fisherman here in Long Island recently stopped by with a bucket full of lobsters in return for Alex saving him bait the previous few weeks. I asked him where they came from, and he was clearly as nonplussed as I was. "They're marching into the Sound, I guess. I don't know where they're coming from." Well. We steamed two and ate them immediately, and I decided to make lobster rolls with the rest.

Anyone with roots in New England knows that there is only one classic way to make a lobster roll: top split bun toasted with butter, and lobster mixed only with mayonnaise, celery, and lemon. There are plenty of variations on the internet, with recipes using curry or mustard or cucumber (shudder). I think classic is best because you can really taste the sweet flavor of the lobster (plus, my dad is from Boston).

The toughest part is shelling the lobsters. A good pair of kitchen shears does an excellent job. It definitely takes longer to shell the lobsters that it does to eat the whole roll!

Combine the lobster, mayonnaise, celery, lemon juice, dill, and salt and pepper. Put in refrigerator to chill for 30 minutes.

Lightly butter the insides of the rolls. In a pan over medium heat, toast the rolls until the insides are golden brown.

Fill the rolls to overflowing with the lobster salad. Serve with lemon wedges.

LOBSTER SALAD

This was my favorite thing to eat when I first moved to Mattituck. I was amazed at the giant bowls of lobster salad at parties and at Alex's house.

LOBSTER SALAD I

Serves 4 as a Main Dish or 8 as an Appetizer

2 cups cooked lobster meat (about three 1 ½ pound lobsters), cut into half-inch pieces

¾ cup mayonnaise

1 teaspoon sesame oil

½ cup chopped red onion

½ cup chopped celery

¼ cup chopped green olives

1 tablespoon chopped dill

Salt and pepper to taste

In large bowl, combine mayonnaise and sesame oil. Add lobster meat and all remaining ingredients and mix well. Serve stuffed into half of an avocado, in a sandwich, or on top of salad greens.

LOBSTER SALAD II

Serves 4 as a Main Dish or 8 as an Appetizer

2 cups cooked lobster meat (about three 1 ½ pound lobsters), cut into half-inch pieces

½ cup ketchup

1 tablespoon horseradish

½ teaspoon hot sauce

Half a lemon, juiced (about 2 tablespoons)

In large bowl combine ketchup, horseradish, hot sauce and lemon juice; whisk well. Add the lobster meat and coat well with the sauce.

MUSSELS

Blue mussels are found throughout the Long Island Sound and in the bays and creeks of Long Island; that's the type that we sell at market. Bank mussels also abound, but they are not commercially harvested for food as far as I know; supposedly they have an unpleasant taste. They are being used by some towns as a way to clean the water (they absorb nitrogen) and to stabilize the shoreline.

Most of the mussels that are commercially harvested on Long Island are wild, and the sets of mussels vary every year as they depend on the weather and other environmental factors, like algae blooms. Some years we have them all year long; some years it gets too hot in the summer and they all die off.

One frequent problem is that the mussels (and to some extent oysters) become infested with pea crabs in the fall. Pea crabs are small, pea-sized parasites that live inside mussels, oysters and clams. They are edible and apparently were a favorite of George Washington, but our customers are pretty grossed out by them across the board. When the mussels have more pea crabs in them than not we stop bringing them in for the rest of the season.

Use local mussels if you can find them; if not, the farm-raised Prince Edward Island mussels are a good alternative. Rinse them under running water and pull off the stringy beards (the byssal thread, which enables them to attach themselves to rocks or pilings). Don't bother to scrub them unless they are really muddy or dirty.

Mussels are cooked a myriad of different ways in different cultures. One of the best recipes I've ever made was simply mussels steamed in beer and dipped in melted butter.

STEAMED MUSSELS WITH BUTTER AND HERBS

Serves 2

3 pounds mussels, cleaned and rinsed, beards removed

1 stick butter (8 tablespoons)

3 cloves garlic, crushed

½ teaspoon salt

1 ½ cups white wine

¼ cup chopped fresh parsley

2 tablespoons chopped fresh thyme

1 loaf of crusty bread

Over medium-low heat, melt butter in dutch oven or heavy pot. Add garlic and salt and cook for 2 to 3 minutes. Add wine and herbs; turn heat to medium-high. Cook for 4 to 5 minutes.

Add mussels to pot, stir. Cover and cook until mussels open, about 4 to 5 minutes.

Serve in bowls with plenty of broth and bread to mop up the juice.

STEAMED MUSSELS WITH WHITE WINE AND CHORIZO

Serves 2

3 pounds mussels, cleaned and rinsed, beards removed

1 tablespoon olive oil

2 links chorizo (3 to 4 ounces), casings removed and diced

Half of a medium red onion, diced (about ½ cup)

3 cloves garlic, slivered

1 ⅓ cups white wine (Chardonnay or Riesling)

1 teaspoon red pepper flakes

2 tablespoons chopped fresh parsley (or cilantro)

1 loaf of crusty bread

Recipe by Jake Henry

Over medium-low heat, add the olive oil to dutch oven or heavy pot; add chorizo. Sauté for 4 minutes until dark brown.

Add onion and garlic; sauté for 2 to 3 minutes.

Add mussels and wine. Add red pepper flakes and chopped parsley. Stir to combine.

Raise heat to medium-high; put lid on pot. Cook for 4 to 5 minutes.

When mussels open, remove pot from heat.

Stir well. Serve in bowls with plenty of sauce, and crusty bread to mop up the juice.

MUSSEL AND CORN CHOWDER

Serves 2 to 4

2 pounds mussels, cleaned
and rinsed, beards removed

3 tablespoons butter

2 shallots, minced

2 ears corn, kernels removed
from cob

1 ½ cups white wine

1 ½ cups plus ¼ cup whole milk
or cream

1 ½ tablespoons flour

2 tablespoons chopped
fresh basil

Salt to taste

Recipe by Chef Robin Puskas

Melt butter over medium heat in a large stockpot.
Add shallots and cook until softened. Add corn and
cook 1 minute more.

Pour in wine and turn heat to high. Bring to a boil
and simmer, uncovered, until wine is reduced by
half, about 5 minutes. Add 1 ½ cup milk and reduce
heat to medium.

Whisk flour into ¼ cup milk. Add a little hot liquid
and whisk again. Pour flour mixture into pot and stir
constantly for 2 to 3 minutes until thickened.

Add mussels and cover. Cook for 4 to 5 minutes
until mussels are just opened, shaking the covered
pot once or twice during the cooking time to stir up
the liquid. Taste and add salt if needed.

Transfer mussels to a shallow bowl and spoon
chowder around them. Garnish with chopped basil
if desired and serve immediately.

MUSSELS WITH MARKET VEGETABLES

Serves 2

1 ½ pounds mussels, cleaned and rinsed, beards removed

2 tablespoons butter

2 garlic cloves, crushed

2 stalks celery, chopped, with leaves (about 1 cup)

½ large shallot, sliced

2 cups white wine

½ to ¾ cup diced tomato

2 cups cooked Basmati rice for serving

2 teaspoons chopped fresh parsley

Recipe by Erika Sipos

Melt butter in heavy pot over medium-low heat. Add garlic, celery, and shallot. Cook until softened, about 6 to 8 minutes.

Add wine and turn heat to medium-high. Add mussels and cover pot. Cook for 4 to 5 minutes. Remove opened mussels to a plate with a slotted spoon.

Add tomato and continue cooking until liquid is reduced by half. You should have about 1 cup of liquid.

Meanwhile, take mussels out of shell. When liquid has reduced, return mussels to pot and heat through.

Serve over bowls of rice. Sprinkle the parsley on top to garnish.

OYSTERS

The Atlantic oyster, found along the coast from Canada to the Gulf of Mexico, is one of 5 different species of oyster worldwide. It has a storied history in the New York area, and is still very popular commercially today.

While there are plenty of wild sets of oysters around Long Island, in recent years aquaculture has exploded on the East End. According to the 2016 Long Island Sound Study, "From 2012 to 2014, New York's oyster harvest increased by more than 370 percent, in part due to increased aquaculture production."

The increased presence of oysters in the waters of Long Island Sound and the nearby creeks and bays highlight the "socioeconomic importance of this species to Long Island," (2016 Long Island Sound Study) and is a positive indication of the water quality. Oysters filter the water, removing algae and excess nutrients from the water. Farming oysters provides habitat for marine organisms, and oyster beds stabilize coastal sediments and help minimize impacts from storm surges (from NOAA's Fishwatch: U.S. Seafood Facts).

The oysters here in Long Island have a particularly briny flavor; the salinity, alkalinity, mineral content, and temperature of the water have a decided effect on the oysters' taste. The word "merroir" has recently been used to describe the local conditions that produce a particular oyster's flavor, much as "terroir" refers to the taste of a wine imparted by the environment in which it is produced.

Probably the most popular notion among customers at the fish stand is that old saw that says you should never eat oysters in months that don't have an "R" in them (May, June, July, August). Since refrigeration, that adage doesn't hold true. We usually carry steamer clams in those spring and summer months instead of oysters, which spawn in the summer, sometimes making them watery and not as plump and tasty.

Methods of cooking oysters are endless, from simply eating them raw to elaborate preparations such as Oysters Rockefeller. Here are some very simple ideas for eating them on the half shell or roasted in the oven.

MIGNONETTE SAUCES

Raw oysters are usually served on a bed of crushed ice or dampened rock salt in order to hold them steady on the plate, along with various sauces. A common preparation is cocktail sauce and lemon; we like them with hot sauce and horseradish as well.

A traditional mignonette sauce is made with vinegar, shallots or onions, and black pepper. Here are three different mignonettes to try with our fresh raw oysters. Recent guests liked these so much we kept the leftovers to use on fish and meat the next day.

CLASSIC MIGNONETTE

½ cup red wine vinegar

2 tablespoons finely minced shallots

½ teaspoon freshly ground black pepper

GREEN APPLE MIGNONETTE

½ cup rice vinegar

4 tablespoons finely minced granny smith apple

1 tablespoon lime juice

1 tablespoon chopped fresh chives

1 teaspoon sugar

½ teaspoon salt

CUCUMBER MIGNONETTE

½ cup white wine vinegar

5 tablespoons finely minced English cucumber

1 tablespoon finely minced shallot

1 tablespoon chopped fresh cilantro

½ teaspoon salt

Mix all ingredients well. Chill for 30 minutes to let flavors meld.
Spoon on oysters and serve.

A note on eating raw shellfish

New York State has strict rules for harvesting oysters, from the moment they are taken out of certified waters to handling, shipping, and storing them. Harvesters must have a shellfish license and must tag each bag of oysters with the date, time, area, name and license number of the harvester, and the quantity collected. All shellfish must be immediately tagged so that their provenance can be traced in case of contamination.

I have no problem eating raw oysters from the Northeast, or from other parts of the country at a reputable restaurant, except for the Gulf Coast area. Alex and I stopped eating raw shellfish from Florida, Alabama, Louisiana and Texas after many reports of red tides in the Gulf, a type of algae which can have a paralytic effect on anyone who ingests it. We feel that the water is just too warm in these areas and that can encourage the growth of bacteria such as vibrio vulnificus, an extremely dangerous bacteria that will give you nightmares the more you read about it.

Anyone who has a compromised immune system should think twice about eating raw shellfish; ingesting this bacteria can be life-threatening. That being said, we do eat cooked shellfish from the Gulf Coast, such as when baked or fried in a po' boy. Shellfish from colder waters is safer, and has a more appealing briny taste, in my opinion. If there is any question that the shellfish you are being served has not been handled properly, avoid it.

Roast oysters

We sell a lot of oysters at the fish stand; while some folks are confident in their shucking skills, most are very intimidated by prying them open with a sharp knife.

At the fish stand I give out a simple roast oyster recipe that I was forced to use once upon a time. We had a couple dozen oysters for dinner and for some reason Alex was not around to open them. I had no idea how to open them myself at the time and was faced with the dilemma of how to turn a pile of oysters into dinner.

The trick is to use a very hot, 500 degree oven. After a few minutes the shells will start to open slightly, enabling you to insert a knife and remove the top shell. Top the oyster with whatever you like, put it back in the hot oven, and before you know it dinner is ready. That night we ended up scarfing down every oyster, and they were so delicious that I recited the recipe to our customers for years afterward.

Roasted oysters are best in the fall and winter when the weather is cold and the oysters aren't spawning. When the water is cold our local oysters have a superior flavor.

Here is our classic recipe, along with one using tarragon butter. Feel free to experiment with other types of compound butters or sauces; pesto makes a good roast oyster as well.

For a main course, we use 6 to 9 oysters per person. Use 3 per person for an appetizer.

To prepare oysters for roasting

Wash each oyster under cool running water and put on a plate. Notice that each oyster has a cupped side and a flat side; put the cupped side down, so that when the top shell is removed the oyster liquor stays in the bottom shell.

Preheat your oven to 500 degrees. Line a baking sheet with rock salt, or a crumpled sheet of aluminum foil.

Arrange the oysters cupped side down on the baking sheet. When your oven is hot, roast the oyster for a few minutes.

After 3 minutes, check the baking sheet and remove any shells that are starting to open, being sure not to spill the oyster liquor. Keep checking the oysters every minute or two; the oysters will all open at different rates, and you want to remove them quickly so they don't cook too much. Some of them will take a surprisingly long time to open.

When you have removed all the slightly opened oyster shells from the heat, insert your oyster knife in between the shells and work the knife around to the back hinge. Gently remove the top shell, and use your knife to cut the oyster free from the bottom shell.

Rearrange the oysters on the baking sheet, taking care not to spill the liquor.

Top each oyster with your choice of filling; put the baking sheet back in the 500 degree oven and roast for 5 minutes.

ROAST OYSTERS WITH GARLIC AND BACON

Makes enough for one dozen oysters

12 oysters

2 strips of bacon

3 tablespoons olive oil

2 large cloves garlic, chopped

2 tablespoons chopped fresh parsley

Black pepper to taste

In a small pan, fry the bacon 1 to 2 minutes on each side, but remove from the heat before it is completely cooked. Drain on paper towels and roughly chop.

In a small bowl mix the olive oil, garlic, parsley, and fresh pepper.

When you have removed the top shell from the oysters and arranged them on a baking sheet, put a spoonful of the olive oil mixture on each oyster. Top each oyster with two pieces of the partially cooked bacon.

Put oysters back in the 500 degree oven and cook for 2 to 3 minutes; do not overcook.

ROAST OYSTERS WITH TARRAGON BUTTER

Makes enough for one dozen oysters

12 oysters

For the Tarragon Butter

¼ pound (one stick) plus 1 tablespoon unsalted butter, softened

2 tablespoons diced shallots

½ cup white wine

1 tablespoon chopped fresh tarragon

Salt and freshly ground pepper to taste

For the Tarragon Butter:

Sauté the shallots over medium-low heat in one tablespoon butter, about 1 to 2 minutes. Add the wine and raise heat to medium.

Reduce the wine until the pan is almost dry. Add tarragon to the pan and mix well; remove from heat. Let mixture cool.

In a medium bowl add the tarragon mixture to the softened butter. Mix thoroughly; add salt and freshly ground pepper to taste.

Using parchment paper or plastic wrap, form butter into a log and wrap tightly. Refrigerate for 2 to 3 hours or freeze and use as needed.

For the Oysters:

When you have removed the top shell from the oysters and arranged them on a baking sheet, remove tarragon butter from the refrigerator or freezer and unwrap. Slice several pats of butter from the log (it doesn't matter if the pats fall apart). Put a piece or two of the tarragon butter on each oyster.

Put oysters back in the 500 degree oven and cook for 2 to 3 minutes; do not overcook.

SCALLOPS

Long Island is loaded with scallops. Sea scallops are found offshore in large beds, and are harvested with scallop dredges; bay scallops, found in Peconic Bay and other small local coves, are harvested with dredges, tongs or hand rakes. You will very rarely find anyone diving for scallops in the North Atlantic —I always laugh when I see that on the menu. "Diver scallops" is a marketing term, although there is a small diver scallop fishery in Maine in the summer.

Sea scallops are larger and have a large smooth white shell. Bays are smaller and have a cork-shaped meat and a small, gray, ridged shell. Peconic Bay scallops are rightfully famous, super sweet and super expensive. While sea scallops are harvested all year long, bays have a short season from November to March, to ensure that the scallops reproduce.

We sell both types at the fish stand. Bay scallops used to be so plentiful that Alex used to sell them for $6 a pound. After a severe brown tide, which caused almost all of the bay scallops to die off, we didn't sell them for at least 15 years. After lots of work reseeding the bay, the scallops came back, but in much fewer numbers. Now the average price is $22-25 a pound. I have had customers report that Peconic Bay scallops are selling for up to $45 a pound in Manhattan fish markets!

Sea scallops are plentiful and well-managed; they have been surveyed yearly since 1979. Nowadays NOAA's Northeast Fisheries Science Center uses underwater cameras to supplement the data.

Bay scallop populations are directly tied to the health of our bays; in recent years the harvest has been low due to brown or rust tides, which are algae blooms that kill small shellfish and the eelgrass that is their habitat. Cornell Cooperative Extension runs a SPAT program (Suffolk Project in Aquaculture Training), where volunteers help reseed the bays with tiny scallops and oysters.

Both of the types of scallops we sell can be eaten raw; both freeze very well. If you get a chance to try the Peconic Bay scallops, I promise you they are worth splurging on!

GRILLED SCALLOP SALAD WITH BASIL VINAIGRETTE

Serves 4

For the Scallops

1 ½ pounds sea scallops, tough adductor muscle removed, rinsed and patted dry

3 medium white onions, quartered

1 pint cherry tomatoes, washed

Salt and pepper to taste

For the Vinaigrette

1 cup fresh basil leaves, washed

¼ cup olive oil

3 tablespoons white wine vinegar

1 medium garlic clove

½ teaspoon salt

¼ teaspoon pepper

For the Vinaigrette:

To make a vinaigrette, combine all ingredients and process in food processor. Add a little more olive oil if you feel it's necessary; taste and adjust seasonings.

Store in a tightly closed jar in refrigerator.

For the Scallops:

Soak 10 to 12 wooden skewers in water for about 30 minutes before assembling kabobs.

Carefully pierce one scallop with two skewers, about ½ inch apart. Add scallops to the two skewers so you have about 5 or 6 scallops on each pair of skewers.

Skewer all the scallops and place them on a platter or large plate. Season with salt and pepper.

Skewer the onion quarters and cherry tomatoes, alternating each on the skewer.

Prepare a grill. Cook the scallop and vegetable skewers about 2 to 3 minutes per side.

Take scallops and vegetables off skewers and put in a large bowl. Pour the vinaigrette over the scallops and vegetables and gently toss.

SCALLOP GRATIN

A perfect scallop is a beautiful thing —but what about a broken one? I like to sell my customers nice whole scallops, so I often spend a lot of time picking out pieces that were sliced up by an overeager knife. Sometimes I bring home a bagful wondering what I can do with them for dinner.

Scallop cakes are a good solution, but lately I've noticed little prepackaged shells stuffed with scallops at our fillet house. They are sold frozen and make a delicious (and easy) appetizer or quick lunch. The ones in the store were a little too bready for our taste, so I decided to make my own.

If you have scallop pieces you can use those; otherwise chop the scallops roughly into ¼ inch pieces. Be sure to remove the tough, rectangular muscle found on the side of the scallop and discard.

I washed and reused the shells from the stuffed scallops I bought; you can do the same or buy empty shells at a housewares store. For a slightly larger serving of the gratin, use six ounce ramekins.

The great thing about gratins is you can make them ahead of time, freeze them and have them ready whenever you want a quick meal.

SCALLOP GRATIN I

Serves 4

2 cups chopped sea scallops, tough muscle removed

½ stick butter, softened (4 tablespoons)

2 tablespoons chopped scallions

4 cloves garlic, minced

1 tablespoon chopped bacon

1 tablespoon lemon juice

1 tablespoon chopped fresh parsley

¼ cup plain bread crumbs

⅛ teaspoon paprika

Mix all ingredients. Put about ¼ cup of the mixture in each ungreased shell (you should have enough for 8 shells or 4 6-ounce ramekins)

Put the shells on a baking sheet. Bake at 425 degrees for 10 to 12 minutes. If you like, put the gratins under the broiler for 2 to 3 minutes to brown the top.

SCALLOP GRATIN II

Serves 4

2 cups chopped sea scallops, tough muscle removed

1 stick butter, softened (¼ cup)

1 lemon, zested

2 tablespoons minced chives

4 cloves garlic, minced

2 teaspoons minced fresh oregano

Salt and pepper to taste

4 teaspoons panko

Mix all ingredients except the panko together. Put about ½ cup of the mixture into a 6-ounce, ungreased ramekin (you should have enough for 4 ramekins).

Put the ramekins on a baking sheet. Sprinkle each with 1 teaspoon of panko.

Bake at 425 degrees for 10 minutes. If you like, put the gratins under the broiler for 2 to 3 minutes to brown the top.

KEVIN'S FISH AND SCALLOP CEVICHE

Serves 4 to 6 as an Appetizer

1 pound combination of scallops and firm white fish (we used fluke fillet)

7 limes, juiced

1 orange, juiced

1 tablespoon salt

1 red onion, sliced as thinly as possible

1 red pepper, diced

1 can of corn, drained and rinsed

1 bunch of fresh cilantro, minced

Paprika to taste

3 cloves garlic, minced (optional)

Tortilla chips (optional)

Juice the limes and orange. Strain and refrigerate in a non-reactive bowl until ready to add ingredients.

Remove and discard the tough muscle on the side of each scallop and cut scallops into cubes (about ½ to ¾ inch). Cut the fish fillet into strips, making sure the flesh contains no bones, and cut fish into cubes about the same size as the scallops.

Combine the scallops and fish with the lime and orange juice; it should be swimming in the bowl. If not, make more juice. Add the salt, then refrigerate for 3 hours.

Add the onion, pepper, corn, cilantro and paprika (and garlic if using). Continue to refrigerate for at least another hour.

Serve cold or at room temperature, with tortilla chips.

Note: if you double, triple or otherwise multiply the amount of fish in this recipe, don't add more than two tablespoons of salt during marination.

STEPH'S FISH AND SCALLOP CEVICHE

Serves 8 to 10 as an Appetizer

2 pounds combination of scallops and firm white fish (we used fluke and sea bass)

3 cups fresh lemon juice

1 medium red onion, diced (about 1 cup)

⅔ cup chopped fresh cilantro

2 tablespoons chopped jalapeño, seeds removed

1 teaspoon salt

½ cup chopped tomato (optional)

Juice the lemons. Strain and refrigerate in a non-reactive bowl until ready to add ingredients.

Remove and discard the tough muscle on the side of each scallop and cut scallops into cubes (about ½ to ¾ inch). Cut the white fish and the sea bass into strips, making sure the flesh contains no bones, then cut fish into cubes about the same size as the scallops.

Combine the scallops and fish with the lemon juice; it should be swimming in the bowl. If not, make more juice. Refrigerate for 3 hours.

Remove from the refrigerator and drain the liquid using a colander. Put the fish and scallops back in the bowl.

Add the onion, cilantro, jalapeño, and salt (and tomato if using). Serve cold or at room temperature.

SCALLOP CEVICHE

Serves 4 to 6 as an Appetizer

1 pound sea scallops, tough muscle removed, rinsed and patted dry

1 lemon, juiced

1 orange, juiced

2 limes, juiced

3 scallions, chopped (both white and green parts)

3 tablespoons finely diced red bell pepper

3 tablespoons chopped fresh cilantro

2 to 2 ½ tablespoons finely diced jalapeño pepper

Cayenne pepper (optional)

Cut the scallops into quarters or eighths, depending on their size (you should have bite-sized pieces). Put in a large bowl.

Juice the lemon, orange and limes and pour the juice over the scallops. You should have about 1 cup of juice; the scallops should be completely covered.

Add the scallions, bell pepper, cilantro and jalapeño to the scallops. Gently stir to combine.

Cover and refrigerate for at least 1 hour.

Serve in a bowl with chips, or on individual plates or in glasses. Dust with the cayenne pepper if desired.

Note: Marinating the scallops anywhere from 30 minutes to 2 hours is ideal. We routinely marinate several more hours, which cures the scallops to a slightly different texture. As this is a personal preference, we suggest you experiment and find the marination time that works for you. Any leftovers can be refrigerated and eaten the next day.

SEARED SCALLOPS WITH SORREL SAUCE

Serves 2 as a Main Dish or 4 as an Appetizer

1 pound sea scallops, tough muscle removed, rinsed and patted dry

1 tablespoon olive oil or grapeseed oil

Lemon wedges

For the Sorrel Sauce:

1 tablespoon olive oil

½ medium white onion, diced

2 cloves garlic, minced

1 bunch sorrel, stems trimmed, leaves washed and chopped (4 to 5 cups)

1 ½ cups chicken stock

¼ cup heavy cream

Recipe by Chef/Farmer Ray Bradley

At the market in the spring, the farmers sell beautiful bunches of sorrel, a spinach-like green. It is slightly bitter and has a lemony flavor. My farmer friend Ray Bradley (trained by an old-school French chef in cooking school) gave me this recipe years ago when I asked what I could do with his sorrel. It also makes a great sauce with a white fish, like flounder, cod or blackfish.

For the Sorrel Sauce:

Heat the oil in a large saucepan over medium-low heat. Add the onion and garlic and cook until softened, about 4 to 5 minutes.

Add the chopped sorrel to the pan. Cook for one minute. Add the chicken stock to the pan and turn heat to medium-high.

Cook until the sorrel is wilted and the liquid is reduced, about 4 to 5 minutes.

Stir in the heavy cream. Remove from heat and let cool. When cool, pour into a blender or food processor and puree.

For the Scallops:

Season the scallops with salt and pepper on each side.

Heat the oil in a large skillet over high heat. When the pan is hot, put the scallops in without crowding. Let the scallops cook for 2 minutes without disturbing them in the pan. Turn over and cook for 1 minute more.

To serve, spoon sauce on a serving plate and arrange scallops on top. Serve with fresh lemon slices.

LAING'S SCALLOP SASHIMI WITH LEMON AND ORANGE ZEST

Serves 6 as an Appetizer

1 ¼ pound sea scallops, tough muscle removed, sliced in very thin rounds

1 English cucumber, sliced in very thin rounds

Sea salt and freshly ground pepper

½ jalapeño pepper (optional)

1 lemon, washed and cut in half

1 orange, washed and cut in half

3 tablespoons chopped fresh cilantro

Mint sprig for garnish

For the Garlic and Ginger Oil

1 cup vegetable oil

2-inch piece of ginger, peeled and chopped

1 head of garlic, peeled and chopped

Recipe by Laing Laing Wan

For the Garlic and Ginger Oil:

Heat the oil over medium-low heat. Sauté the ginger and garlic until golden brown, about 3 to 4 minutes. Cool. Store in a tightly covered container in the refrigerator.

For the Scallop Sashimi:

Overlap the scallops and cucumbers on a plate to make a pattern. Sprinkle with sea salt and fresh pepper.

If using the jalapeño, layer over the scallops and cucumbers.

Juice half of the lemon and half of the orange. Sprinkle 2 tablespoons of the lemon juice and 2 tablespoons of the orange juice over the scallops.

Grate lemon zest from remaining half of the lemon and orange zest from remaining half of the orange over the scallops.

Sprinkle 2 tablespoons Garlic and Ginger Oil over the scallops.

Sprinkle the cilantro over the scallops.

Decorate the plate with one section of peeled orange and the sprig of mint.

ERIKA'S MARINATED SEA SCALLOPS

Serves 4 to 6 as an Appetizer

6 large sea scallops (about ½ pound), tough muscle removed

1 tablespoon mayonnaise

1 teaspoon sesame oil

½ teaspoon lemon juice

½ teaspoon chili oil

Pinch kosher salt

Black sesame seeds for garnish

Persian cucumbers or rice crackers for serving

Recipe by Erika Sipos

This recipe comes from our good friend Erika, whom we met working at the market over 25 years ago. She says these marinated scallops are perfect on a hot day with a glass of rosé. It is also great made with bay scallops.

Rinse the scallops and pat dry. Slice them into thin matchsticks, then turn them and slice into small cubes (about ⅛ to ¼ inch each).

Gently mix the scallop cubes with the mayonnaise, sesame oil, lemon juice, chili oil and salt.

Slice the cucumbers on the diagonal into discs, about ⅛ to ¼ inch thick. Put a dollop of the scallop mixture on each disc, and top with a sprinkling of sesame seeds.

Alternatively, serve the scallops as a dip with rice crackers on the side.

SHRIMP

Key West used to be loaded with shrimp boats; when Alex and I first started visiting twenty years ago, the harbor (called Key West Bight) was full of them. As the waterfront got more and more gentrified, the shrimp boats were forced out and moved to Stock Island, Key West's low-rent neighbor. What is left of the shrimp fleet remains there. You still see plenty of local boats in Florida, and even a few from Alabama and Texas, but the fleet is a fraction of its former self.

Key West is still the biggest fishing port in Florida, and it has landed on the top ten list for shrimp value several times over the past twenty years. Fishermen here have had to deal with hurricanes, the BP oil spill, and increasingly tight fishing regulations. Certain areas of the local waters are designated as no-fish areas, like the Tortugas Ecological Reserve, and there are several research and wildlife refuge areas. There is also an amendment to the state constitution that prohibits fishermen from using nets to catch fish in the state of Florida.

There are several types of shrimp that are caught off of South Florida, including pink, brown, white, royal red, and rock shrimp. Key West is known for its famous Key West pinks, locally known as "pink gold."

If you are lucky enough to be visiting the Florida Keys, you can usually get fresh shrimp and certainly fresh Key West pinks —ask for them by name. You can find them fresh in the local fish markets and most of the local grocery stores at a decent price.

Outside of the states bordering the Gulf of Mexico, it is almost impossible to find fresh shrimp, as they are highly perishable. Often the shrimp are flash frozen on board the shrimp boats and are only available that way.

If possible you should buy American-caught wild Gulf shrimp. We think the next best choice is wild Mexican shrimp. Avoid the farm raised versions from Asia; they are raised in filthy conditions by people paid slave wages (or who are actual slaves). One way you can tell is by the price. Wild shrimp caught responsibly will always cost more, and in this case, it is worth it to pay more.

Shrimp sizes vary; wholesale sizing is done by the count of shrimp per pound, like 16/20, 21/25 or 26/30. You will pay more for the big shrimp. In the local seafood markets or supermarkets they are just called jumbo, extra large, large, and medium. Unless you need a particular size for a recipe, I just buy whatever looks freshest. Look for bright pink, sweet-smelling shrimp with firm, hard shells.

SHRIMP SCAMPI

Serves 4

1 ½ to 2 pounds shrimp, cleaned and deveined

½ cup butter (4 tablespoons)

2 tablespoons olive oil

4 cloves garlic, minced

4 tablespoons chopped fresh parsley

Juice from half a lemon (about 2 tablespoons)

My Italian father-in-law lived with us in Mattituck for some time, and we often made this simple dish. He always made it the same way with lots of garlic and fresh parsley.

Add a splash of white wine to the pan, or a teaspoon of crushed red pepper, or two tablespoons of pesto to change the recipe as you like.

In a large pan, heat the butter and the oil over medium heat. Add the garlic and sauté for one minute. Add the shrimp and stir to coat. Cook for 2 minutes.

Turn the shrimp and cook for another minute or two depending on their size. Remove from the heat and stir in the parsley and the lemon juice. Serve over pasta or rice, or as is with crusty bread.

SHRIMP TACOS

Serves 4

1 to 1 ½ pounds shrimp (use 21/25 per pound or slightly smaller)

3 to 4 tablespoons prepared crab boil

1 lemon, cut in half

2 or 3 bay leaves

For the Sauce:

¼ cup sour cream

2 tablespoons mayonnaise

¼ teaspoon cumin

¼ teaspoon salt

Juice of 1 lime

10 to 12 small corn or flour tortillas

For the Filling:

2 cups red or green cabbage, sliced thinly

1 cup avocado, cut in 1-inch chunks

1 jalapeño pepper, sliced (either pickled or fresh)

4 tablespoons chopped fresh cilantro

Lime wedges

Great shrimp tacos can be done incredibly simply, using lots of fresh lime juice, a little slaw, and good tortillas. Here I use boiled shrimp, but you can use grilled or breaded shrimp as well.

To a large pot of water add the crab boil, the lemon halves, and the bay leaves and stir. When the water is boiling, add the shrimp. Cook for 2 to 3 minutes depending on the size of the shrimp; when shrimp float to the top of the pot, they are done.

Drain the shrimp in a colander and set in a bowl of ice water. When cool, shell and devein them.

For the Sauce:

Put all sauce ingredients in a small bowl and whisk.

Heat the tortillas in a hot frying pan for a minute or two on a side, or microwave a stack of them between two paper towels for a minute.

Fill tortillas to your liking with the shrimp, cabbage, avocado, jalapeños, cilantro, and sauce. Squeeze a wedge of lime over them before eating.

SHRIMP SALAD

Serves 2

1 pound shrimp, cooked and deveined

⅔ cups chopped celery, with leaves

½ cup chopped black olives

1 teaspoon capers, rinsed and drained

Lemon wedges

Sea salt

For Dressing I:

½ cup mayonnaise

½ cup buttermilk

2 tablespoons chopped fresh cilantro

1 tablespoon lime juice

¼ teaspoon salt

Pepper to taste

For Dressing II:

1 tablespoon Dijon mustard

2 tablespoons white wine vinegar

¼ teaspoon salt

½ cup olive oil

This shrimp salad can be served on top of a green salad, stuffed into half of an avocado, or used in a sandwich. Choose from either of two dressings.

For Dressing I:

Whisk together all ingredients for the dressing. Store in a tightly sealed container.

For Dressing II:

Combine the mustard, vinegar, and salt. Gradually add the oil and whisk together. Store in a tightly sealed container.

For Shrimp:

Chop shrimp into ¼ inch pieces. Add the celery, black olives, and capers and mix well.

Pour just enough of the dressing of your choice over the shrimp salad to coat and toss well.

Squeeze a lemon wedge over the salad and sprinkle with sea salt.

SQUID

We catch a lot of squid off of Long Island. Nearly eight million pounds of loligo (now called longfin) squid were landed in New York State in 2012. Most New Yorkers don't realize that squid is a truly local catch and a very stable fishery. It's also a fish stand staple. Everyone knows calamari: squid rings that are battered, deep fried, and served in nearly every bar and restaurant; but there are many other squid preparations that rival fried calamari. Europeans and Asians seem to be familiar with a wider array of squid recipes than Americans, but with such an abundant, stable fishery, squid's day in the spotlight is not far off.

One of the things we like to do at the fish stand is encourage customers to start cooking outside of their comfort zone. Squid is highly perishable and a bit unfamiliar to most people, thus many customers look upon squid with apprehension. There are really only two rules for dealing with squid: one is for storage, the other is for cooking.

Selection and storage

Since squid is so highly perishable it is very difficult to find fresh squid. Most squid is sold frozen or defrosted and marked "previously frozen." Freezing, though, actually makes squid's texture a little more tender and has no deleterious effects on its taste. That being said, if you can get fresh squid, you need to use it within one day or else put it in the freezer; it will be just fine either way. It's easy to defrost it for a couple of hours in the refrigerator before you cook it.

General cooking advice

The rule for cooking squid is paradoxical. To cook it perfectly, you must do so either very quickly —two minutes or less over high heat— or cook it for a very long while, at least 45 minutes or more. Anywhere in between and you will have some very rubbery, chewy squid. Get the timing right and there is nothing more tender or tasty. We usually use the shorter method, stopping cooking after 1 or 2 minutes at the most. If it's not right, well, there's always the longer way!

At the fish stand we sell cleaned squid, which is ready to cook, or whole squid, which needs to be cleaned before using. Directions for cleaning squid can be found in the How-To section on page 205. If you buy whole squid make sure you get a little extra, as you will lose quite a bit in cleaning.

Can you eat it raw?

Only if it is very, very fresh. It's hard to find exceptionally fresh squid. Fresh squid is very firm; its color is white or a pale pinkish color. If it is soft at all or is a reddish color, it is not fresh enough to eat raw and should be cooked.

TXIKITO'S QUICK SQUID SALAD

Serves 4

2 pounds squid, cleaned

2 tablespoons olive oil

Salt

Juice of one lemon (about 4 tablespoons)

For the Tomato-Squid Vinaigrette:

2 teaspoons high-quality Italian tomato paste

2 teaspoons water

Juice of one lemon (about 4 tablespoons)

Pinch of salt

1 ½ cups good-quality Spanish olive oil

1 cup parsley leaves

1 cup diced peeled tomato

1 cup chopped Kalamata olives

¼ cup toasted pine nuts

Toasted garlic-rubbed bread for serving

Recipe by Chef/Author Alex Raij, Txikito, El Quinto Pino, La Vara, Tekoá, New York City

Cut squid bodies in rough triangles about 1 ½ inches long. Save the tentacles and discard any wings attached to the bodies.

Set a mesh strainer over a bowl. Heat a large sauté pan on medium heat. Add the olive oil and sauté the bodies and the tentacles in batches, seasoning with salt as you go. Brush the squid with lemon juice between batches. Cook for 1 to 2 minutes on each side.

Transfer the squid to the prepared strainer to catch the juices.

For the Tomato-Squid Vinaigrette:

In a blender combine tomato paste, water, lemon juice and salt. Turn the motor on medium-low and add the olive oil in a thin stream. Add the reserved squid juices in a thin stream. Taste and adjust seasoning.

In a large bowl combine the sautéed squid, the parsley leaves, diced peeled tomato and the chopped olives. Toss with enough tomato-squid vinaigrette to coat. Top with the toasted pine nuts.

Serve with toasted garlic-rubbed bread.

COLD SQUID SALAD

Serves 6

2 pounds squid, cleaned, with tubes cut into rings and large tentacles cut in half

1 cup red pepper, sliced in strips

½ cup chopped red onion

½ cup chopped celery (about 2 stalks)

½ cup green olives, sliced in half

⅓ cup chopped fresh parsley

¼ cup good olive oil

4 tablespoons apple cider vinegar

4 tablespoons lemon juice

1 teaspoon garlic, minced

1 teaspoon salt

½ teaspoon black pepper

½ teaspoon red pepper flakes

Bring a large pot of salted water to a boil. Add the squid to the pot. When water comes to a second boil set a timer for 2 minutes.

After 2 minutes remove pot from heat and pour squid into a colander. Rinse the squid with cold water.

Place in a large bowl. Add the rest of the ingredients and mix well. Taste and adjust seasoning.

GRILLED SQUID

Serves 4

1 ½ to 2 pounds cleaned squid, tubes left whole

3 tablespoons olive oil

1 lemon, juiced

3 to 4 tablespoons chopped fresh herbs (use any combination of mint, basil, or parsley)

Salt and pepper

Lemon wedges

This is one of those very simple recipes that results in a delicious dish. Buy some squid for the next time you are grilling and try it.

Put squid in a bowl and drizzle the olive oil over it. Add the lemon juice and the fresh herbs and season with salt and pepper. Mix well.

Prepare a cleaned and oiled grill (you may elect to use an oiled grill basket if you like). When grill is hot put the squid on and grill one minute per side. Do not overcook.

Serve immediately, with lemon wedges.

SEAFOOD FRA DIAVOLO

Serves 4

½ pound squid, cleaned, with squid bodies cut into rings

½ pound scallops, with tough muscle removed

2 tablespoons olive oil

1 medium yellow onion, sliced (about 3 cups)

2 cloves garlic, chopped

1 ½ to 2 pounds tomatoes, chopped

¾ cup white wine

¼ cup chopped fresh basil

¼ cup chopped fresh parsley

½ teaspoon red pepper flakes

Fra Diavolo ("Brother Devil") is a spicy sauce for seafood, usually served over linguine. You can make it with lobster, shrimp, scallops, scungilli, mussels, squid, or any combination thereof. This recipe uses squid and scallops, but feel free to improvise. Make it as hot (or not) as you like.

Heat olive oil in a stockpot on medium-low. Add the onion and garlic and cook until soft, about 10 minutes.

Add the tomatoes, wine, basil, parsley, and red pepper flakes and stir. Turn heat up and bring to a boil.

Simmer and let cook for 30 minutes, stirring occasionally, until sauce cooks down.

Add scallops and squid; as soon as they are heated through, about 2 minutes, turn off heat.

Serve over linguine or as is.

STONE CRAB

Stone crab is fished commercially throughout the Florida Keys. It is super sweet and yields big snowy white chunks of meat. The orange and white shell is very hard, and the tips of the claws (the only part of the crab that is eaten) are black. The commercial season runs from October to May.

Fishermen catch stone crabs in pots baited with pigs' feet and set on both the ocean side and the gulf side of the Keys. The pot is raised out of the water using a hauler. The crabs inside are removed and one crab claw is broken off and kept (both claws are allowed to be harvested if they are of legal size —2 ¾ inches), then the crab is thrown back into the sea. The crabs are able to regenerate their claws and thus get caught over and over again.

Stone crabs are prized, and restaurant prices in Key West and Miami are insanely high —sometimes the price is by the ounce. You can save quite a bit of money if you go to a local seafood market and buy them there. In early 2015, jumbo crab claws at the seafood market sold for $33 to $38 per pound, and large claws for $23 to $28 per pound.

Stone crab must be cooked as soon as it comes off the boat; if not, the meat will stick to the shell and will be nearly impossible to remove. For that reason, the crab catch on the boat is not iced, and the crabs are cooked immediately upon return to the dock. When you buy stone crab from the seafood market it has already been cooked; you just need to steam the claws in a pot of boiling water for a few minutes to warm them up.

How To Cook Stone Crabs

If you are lucky enough to get a batch of fresh stone crab claws, here is the procedure for cooking them.

Bring a large pot of salted water to a boil. Add the stone crabs (anywhere from 1 to 5 pounds). When the pot returns to a boil, set a timer for 5 minutes. We don't add anything to the boiling water, but you may add a commercial crab boil mixture if you like.

After 5 minutes, turn off the heat, and carefully dump the pot of claws into the sink. Immediately cover the claws with ice.

When the claws cool, collect them from the sink and put them in a bowl.

Alex likes to pre-crack the claws before they are served, a necessary step if you've ever tried to crack the rock-hard shells. We have a special stone tool for this, but you can use a heavy wooden mallet or a regular hammer. This is best done outside as the shells tend to go flying.

When the shells are cracked, serve them to guests with a dipping sauce. We usually provide some additional tools —lobster crackers or nutcrackers, and small picks to get the meat out of the far reaches of the shell. The work is worth it; I think the sweet meat tastes better than lobster.

KEY LIME MUSTARD SAUCE

8 tablespoons mayonnaise

8 teaspoons Dijon mustard

3 tablespoons fresh key lime juice

Salt and pepper to taste

This is our standard sauce for crabs. If you don't have key limes, use regular limes.

Combine the mayonnaise and mustard in a bowl. Add the fresh lime juice and whisk. Add salt and pepper to taste.

Divide among several small bowls so each of your guests has one, or just have one big bowl for the table.

RICH MUSTARD SAUCE

½ cup sour cream

1 ½ tablespoons prepared mustard

2 teaspoons melted butter

½ teaspoon parsley flakes

⅛ teaspoon salt

Combine all ingredients. Stir over low heat until just warm. Do not boil.

Divide among several small bowls so each of your guests has one, or just have one big bowl for the table.

SALTY STORIES FROM CAPTAIN ALEX

Captain Alex Villani has fished in different areas of Long Island, from the Great South Bay to Peconic Bay, to the Sound and far offshore. A lot of stories spring from forty-four years of working on the water, mostly the kind best shared over a drink. Here are a few stories straight from Captain Alex to you. So crack open a beer or pour yourself a rum drink and imagine yourself sitting at a dockside bar with your fisherman . . .

"Offshore we fished for lobsters in the summer with sixty pot trawls. It was beautiful being a hundred miles out on the ocean, in anywhere from a hundred and fifty to five hundred feet of water. When we got hot we'd jump overboard and go swimming, and it was amazing —but we'd always leave one man on the boat on watch duty. One time we were in the water and the man onboard started frantically waving us in. We swam for the boat, climbed aboard, and when we were all safely on we looked down to see three giant hammerhead sharks circling in the water below us."

"Back in the 80s, Greenport was a pretty tough fishing town. When the scallopers came back to port, they were flush because they had just gotten paid; they went drinking in places like the Whiskey Wind and the Rhumb Line. One night while getting rowdy at the bar, an old fisherman popped out his glass eye and rolled it down the length of the bar, through spilled beer and guys doing shots. That shut everyone up for a minute!"

"This one happened last year. One of our fisherman friends Richie was out in Montauk shark fishing. He was right off the beach, and had been catching lots of small great white sharks and throwing them back one after one —you aren't allowed to keep them. Right after he'd tossed another great white back into the water, a girl on one of those stand up paddleboards came right up to the side of the boat. 'Hi,' she said. 'I'm from Pennsylvania. We're staying in Montauk for the summer!' 'That's great,' Richie said. 'Welcome. Do you know that there are sharks out here?' Of course she had no idea. She asked, 'Should I head to shore?' Richie said, 'Yes, go back now,' while trying not to scare her. She paddled off and made it safely to shore. He had thrown twelve young five-foot great whites back in the water right where she had been."

"There's this place called The Caffrey House. It's an old boardinghouse in East Quogue that dates from the 1880s. It was run by one of the original families of the area, and is right on Tiana Bay.

"Back in the late 70s, I moved there by boat and stayed in the Caffrey House while I looked for work on a fishing boat. The proprietor (who is still there today) had a couple of beautiful wooden Chris Craft boats and a collection of jukeboxes and vintage sound equipment (later used in the movie "Private Parts"). There was a huge barn filled with old Stickley furniture and a beautiful white Jaguar and tons of junk all over the place. There was a dog that drank beer also.

"The Caffrey House was a pretty well-known local place for people to hang out, dock their boats, and have a drink at the bar. While I lived there I turned 30 and threw a huge birthday party. It got pretty out of hand, with lots of drinking, loud music, and a huge grill full of lobsters. I don't remember much about that party, except that the next day my friends and I were recovering in some chairs outside when an old man walked up the driveway. He had a live lobster in his hand —or a barely alive one, I should say. He came up to me and asked, "Is this yours? I found it at the end of the driveway." I guess one got away from us! We felt so bad we took the lobster down to the water and, figuring it had earned its freedom, threw it in."

SALTY SEA CAPTAINS

Captain Hands

Captain Danny Hands ran a fishing boat, the *Shinnecock I*, and was a friend of Alex's from back when they both fished out of Shinnecock Inlet in the 70s and 80s.

One day, Captain Hands brought up a 17-foot unexploded World War II torpedo in his net. Being the good citizen that he was, the Captain notified the Coast Guard, who in turn called in the Navy. The Navy had him standby on his boat outside Shinnecock Inlet, with a crew and a hold full of fish, until they figured out what to do. Finally the Navy decided to blow it up, since they thought it was too dangerous to bring into the inlet. They ordered the Captain and the crew off the boat. A Navy demolition team sank it, and after all that drama, the torpedo turned out to be a dud.

The Navy promised to reimburse Hands for the cost of the boat, but reneged when he presented them with a claim. His insurance company also turned him down.

With his livelihood sunk as well, Hands got some help from two Long Island politicians, Senator Alfonse D'Amato and Representative George Hochbrueckner. It took an Act of Congress to get the Captain reimbursement for his boat —and in the end it was only half of what he had asked for.

Captain Hate

Captain Hate was what his crew called him. He was a screamer and captain of the first boat Alex worked on offshore. Alex's thought on his first trip: "I'm eighty miles out to sea trapped with this guy!"

Captain Hate was a merchant marine who did a little fishing on the side. When the fishing got good, he quit the merchant marines and jumped in with both feet. He was a hard man but a great seaman and a hard worker. He always took care of the boat, took care of the crew, and took crap from no one.

Captain Hate managed to fix the problem when the engine room flooded with three feet of water while eighty miles offshore, on the edge of the Continental Shelf.

He survived when a big storm came up, with fifteen to twenty foot waves, and the boat was hit by lightning. There was an enormous boom and black burn marks on the mast, but somehow the electronics survived and, thankfully, the crew was okay.

Another time, when the crew moved their lobster pots offshore and most of them were run over and damaged by scallopers, Captain Hate screamed and yelled and beat a lobster pot to smithereens.

Despite all, Alex learned how to run a boat from him, how to splice wire, and the when and where of fishing with nets and pots —things that can only be learned by experience.

Captain Cash

Captain Cash was a little wiry guy who fished a lot, drank hard, and earned his nickname because he liked cash. He was his own man, always doing his own thing and making fun of the big boats —"Dinosaurs," he called them. "With my own small boat whatever I make I keep for myself." He could often be found in Captain Norm's or Callahan's, popular bars that the fishermen frequented, but he always showed up for work the next morning, always worked hard, and always had fun.

Captain Stian

Stian Stiansen was an old fisherman who taught many, many young men the ways of the water. Everyone knew him and respected him. He was Norwegian and was very proud of his heritage. He grew up working on wooden boats and was experienced with all types of fishing gear. Generous with his advice, he never hesitated to invite a young man along on one of his fishing trips.

Stian was known to be a hard worker; he fished six long days per week. He owned four fishing boats over the years, all named after his wife (*Pauline*, *Pauline II*, *Pauline III* and *Pauline IV*).

Alex would run into him occasionally at the fillet house while unloading boxes of fish to be filleted for the market. "Go get 'em, Alex!" Stian said. "Sell that fish! Make a lot of money!" He was happy to see another fisherman doing well.

One Sunday afternoon —it was Mother's Day— Alex got a phone call. He put the phone down and said, "Stian took a big one in the Inlet."

Stian was heading through the Shinnecock Inlet in the afternoon, coming back from a fishing trip when his boat was hit by a big wave which rolled the boat over. His mate, found clinging to a buoy about a mile out to sea, was rescued in rough waters by a brave Sea Tow captain, but Stian didn't make it. His body was recovered from the beach later that day. He was 85 years old. His death brought a wave of sadness from the community. His family and many that knew him noted that he died doing what he loved.

After Stian's death, his nephew expected to inherit his fishing licenses (for fluke, striped bass, crabs, lobster, and conch), which are valuable now because they are licenses that are no longer available. However, the New York State Department of Environmental Conservation denied him the licenses because, even though Stian had filled out the paperwork properly with the DEC, the nephew did not live in the same house as Stian.

This caused a big outcry in the community. The local state senator and state assemblyman sponsored a bill allowing an easier transfer of licenses to family members, which was signed by the Governor, but the law was too late to help Stian's nephew.

BASIC TECHNIQUES
AND HOW-TO'S

A WORD ABOUT KNIVES

For filleting and skinning, you need a long, sharp knife. Some use a thin boning knife, but I prefer one with a wider blade. I have seen it done with a chef's knife, which has too wide of a blade for me. I think it's a matter of personal preference, but do sharpen your knife before you start. We use one-inch wide Dexter boning knives at the fish stand.

For sharpening we use either a sharpening stone or a steel. We have little mini sharpeners all over the place as they are cheap and handy to keep around. I don't know what the cooking professionals' procedures are for keeping their knives sharp, but we sharpen all the time, definitely before every use. Once every year or two we take all the knives to be professionally sharpened.

HOW TO TRIM, SCALE AND GUT FISH

Most fish need to be trimmed and scaled before cooking. This makes for a nicer presentation and keeps you from being speared by fish spines or eating a mouthful of scales.

1. Put fish on a large cutting board. To trim, use kitchen shears or scissors to cut away the spines on the top of the fish, starting at the tail and working towards the head. Remove any small fins on the top, bottom, and sides of the fish.

2. To scale the fish, use a fish scaler, the back of a knife, or even a spoon. Hold the fish by the tail and begin scraping from tail to head. Flip the fish over and scale the other side. This can be done in the sink or inside a plastic bag to catch the scales.

3. To remove the gills, place the fish on its back and cut crosswise across the throat of the fish. Reach under the gill flap and pull out the gill from one side, then the other. Rinse the head with running water.

4. To gut the fish, make a slit in the fish's belly from the gills to the tail. Clear the cavity of any organs (you may elect to save the liver or any roe that is inside the stomach). Rinse the cavity with running water and remove any viscera that remain.

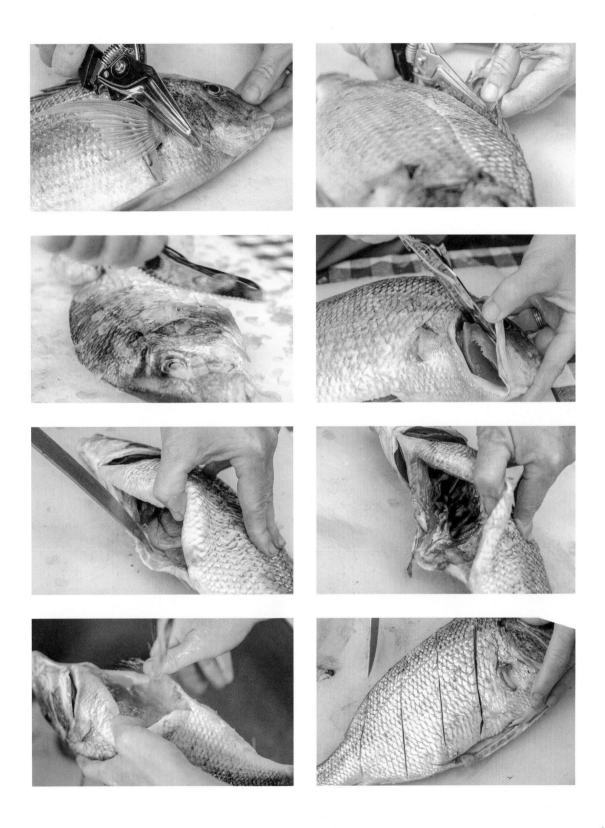

CHAPTER 5: BASIC TECHNIQUES AND HOW-TO'S

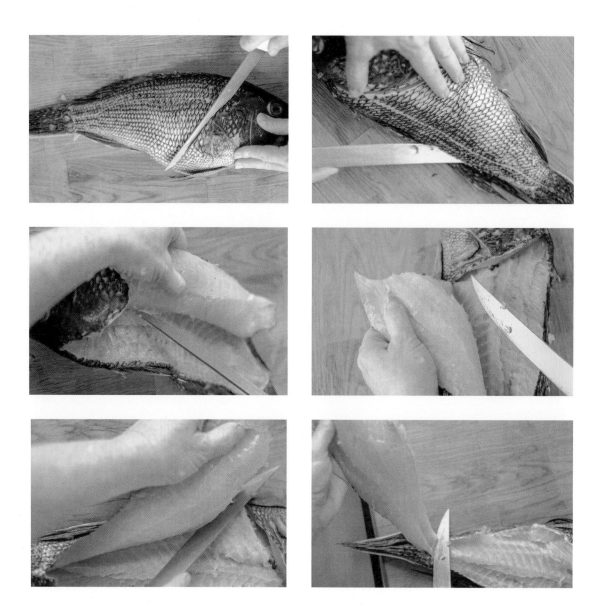

HOW TO FILLET AND SKIN ROUND FISH

This isn't as intimidating as it seems. When Alex taught me, I practiced on bluefish because they were cheap, and it didn't matter if I mangled them. Like anything else, the more you practice the easier it is to do it. Who really cares if you do a sloppy job the first time or two? Make sure you start with a sharp knife.

If you are planning on leaving the skin on while you cook the fish, you need to scale the fish first before you fillet it (see trimming and scaling techniques).

1. Lay the fish facing toward the right, with the back of the fish nearest you. Make a diagonal cut just behind the head from the belly to the back. Press down on the knife so you can feel the fish's backbone.

2. Insert the tip of the knife at the end of the cut you just made and slice along the back of the fish, all the way to the tail. Again, feel the knife against the backbone of the fish.

3. Grasp the flesh of the fish at the end of the cut near the head, and gently pull as you run your knife along the bone, all the way to the tail. Continue slicing the meat away from the bone until most of the fillet lifts off of the fish.

4. Turn the fish around and, starting at the tail, make a cut along the fish's edge from the tail to the belly, being careful not to cut into the stomach sac.

5. Run your knife against the bone until the fillet lifts off. Trim the belly edge of the fillet.

6. Turn the fish over and fillet the other side.

Skinning the Fillets:

1. Lay the fillet skin side down. Cut a small notch into the bottom of the fillet so that you are able to grasp the skin with your left hand (or your right hand, if you are left-handed).

2. While holding the skin on the bottom of the fillet, use your knife to cut away the meat of the fish. Once you get the angle of the knife right, the fillet should easily come off the skin.

3. Turn the fillet over and trim off any remaining pieces of skin.

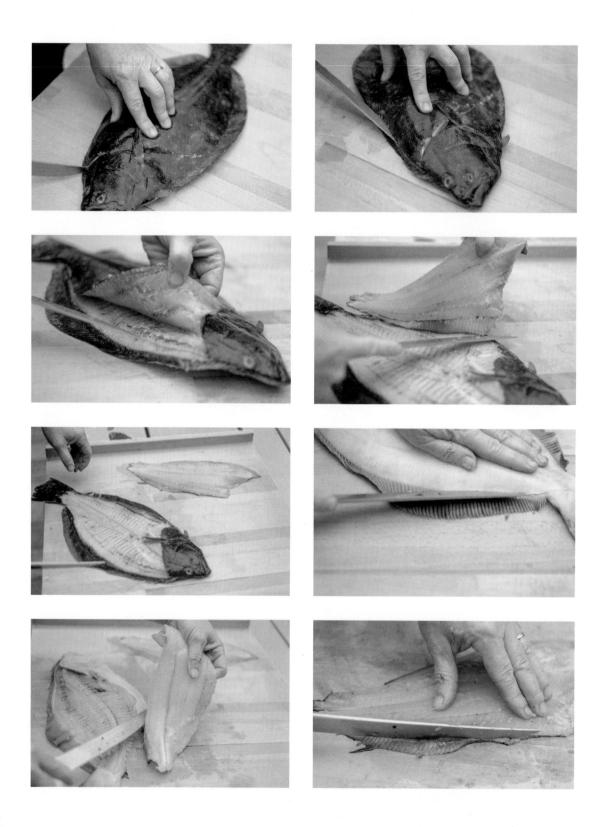

HOW TO FILLET AND SKIN FLATFISH

1. Find the small soft sac that is the fish's stomach, and make your first diagonal cut behind the head, from the belly to the back of the fish.

2. Flatfish have a thin line of meat, called a ribbon, that runs along the top edge of the back of the fish. You will see it when you cut along the edge of the fish all the way to the tail.

3. Proceed from here exactly as when filleting round fish. Insert the tip of the knife at the end of the cut you just made and slice along the back of the fish, all the way to the tail. Feel the knife against the backbone.

4. Grasp the flesh of the fish at the end of the cut near the head, and gently pull as you run your knife along the bone, all the way to the tail. Continue slicing the meat away from the bone until most of the fillet lifts off of the fish.

5. Turn the fish around and, starting at the tail, make a cut along the fish's edge from the tail to the belly, being careful not to cut into the stomach sac.

6. Run your knife against the bone until the fillet lifts off. Trim the belly edge of the fillet.

7. Turn the fish over and fillet the other side.

Skinning the Fillets:

1. The skinning process is exactly the same as for skinning round fish. Lay the fillet skin side down. Cut a small notch into the bottom of the fillet so that you are able to grasp the skin with your left hand (or your right hand, if you are left-handed).

2. While holding the skin on the bottom of the fillet, use your knife to cut away the meat of the fish. Once you get the angle of the knife right, the fillet should easily come off the skin.

3. Turn the fillet over and trim off any remaining pieces of skin. You have the option of slicing the fillets down the center to produce four long, thin fillets.

HOW TO REMOVE PIN BONES

Pin bones are the small line of bones that run through the center of the fish fillet. They don't occur in every species of fish (for example, flounder do not have them), but are apparent in round fish such as sea bass, porgy, salmon, and striped bass.

Pin bones can be removed by cutting the strip of bones out of the fillet. You can either cut the fillet into two thin strips, discarding the line of bones in the center, or carefully cut out the line of bones from the top of the fillet, leaving the two thin strips attached at the bottom in a V-shape.

Alternatively, you may want to pull out the pin bones with tweezers or needle-nose pliers. This makes for a better looking fillet. To do this, lay the fillet on a clean cutting board, skin side down. Start at the thicker top of the fillet and pull out the pin bones one by one. Feel around with your fingers for the next one — they are hard to see. Once you find the right angle to pull them out, it's quite easy.

If you are having trouble finding the pin bones in the fillet, lay the fillet on the bottom of an overturned bowl. This will cause the pin bones to stick out a bit more, making them easier to find and pull.

HOW TO PREPARE MUSSELS

Shellfish need to breathe, so the bag you carry them home in must have a hole or two in it. You may see mussels sold in net bags; that is what the fishermen use to keep the shellfish iced yet allow them to breathe.

Rinse the mussels under running water and scrape any mud off the shell with your fingers. Look for the beard (the stringy material that the mussel uses to anchor itself underwater), pull it off and discard. Some folks scrub mussels with a stiff brush, but I don't find that necessary unless the mussels are excessively dirty.

The mussel shell should be tightly closed. If you find one with a gaping shell, gently tap it with your fingers. If it closes, then it is safe to eat. If not, it is dead; discard it.

To steam the mussels, fill a deep pot with about one inch of liquid; this could be water, beer, wine, or stock. Put the mussels in and steam them until the shells open. I put a lid on the pot but leave it slightly open so the steam can escape. As soon as the mussels open take them off the heat; they are done. Do not overcook!

If you find that one or two mussels have not opened after all the other ones have, discard them.

HOW TO SHUCK CLAMS

It's best if the clams have been sitting still for a while. If the clams have been jostled around too much they tend to clench up their hinge muscle and are tough to open.

1. Use a clam knife or other kitchen knife, but not a sharp one (I use a butter knife with a rounded tip). It's a good idea to wear a glove or use a towel to protect your hand, especially if you are just learning.

2. Hold the clam horizontally in your hand. Put the middle of the knife blade in the center of the lip of the clam and apply steady pressure. The clam should give, and you will be able to wiggle the knife between the two shells.

3. Run your knife all the way around the edges of the clam so that it opens all the way, taking care to save the clam juice (I open them over a bowl to collect any juice that spills). Take the top shell off and discard it.

4. Use your knife to cut the clam loose from the bottom shell.

If you are having a problem opening a few clams, put them in the freezer for 15 minutes. That usually forces the muscle to relax, making it easier to open.

HOW TO PREPARE CLAMS OR OYSTERS

For hard-shell clams and oysters, select shellfish that feel heavy (more meat in the shell) and that are tightly closed. Shellfish need to breathe, so the bag you carry them home in must have a hole or two in it. You may see clams sold in net bags; that is what the fishermen use to keep the shellfish iced yet allow them to breathe.

Rinse the shellfish under running water. If you see an open shell, gently tap it. If it closes, it is safe to use. Discard any with open shells or that smell off in any way.

If you have time, you may want to soak the shellfish. Fill a stockpot with a few quarts of water. Add a half-cup of salt and a half-cup of cornmeal and mix together. Add the clams or oysters. Saltwater is necessary so the shellfish don't die; the cornmeal will irritate the shellfish, causing them to spit out any sand or mud inside.

Refrigerate the pot for an hour or two and let the shellfish purge themselves. Remove the shellfish and rinse under running water. Now they are ready to use. (Note: if you don't have time to soak the shellfish, just rinse under cold water and use as is.)

If you need to store shellfish, take them out of the bag and place them in a bowl, or in a colander set in a bowl. Do not put directly on ice; you may put a damp paper towel on top of them if you like, but I prefer not to. Put them in the back of the refrigerator where it is coldest — as long as the shellfish are cold and can breathe, they will last several days (about 4 to 5 days for hard-shell clams and oysters).

For soft-shell clams, like steamers or razors, select whole clams that are not broken. These types of clams are by nature not tightly closed and may have a tough section of the clam sticking out of the shell. Make sure they are stored in a bag with holes in it until you get home from the market. Soft-shell clams are much more delicate, so take care in handling them. At the fish stand, we treat them as you would a dozen eggs. Don't be surprised if they squirt some water at you while you are handling them; on Long Island they are known as piss clams!

You may use the same soaking method as for clams and oysters. Soft-shell clams tend to retain more sand, so be aware before you add them to a soup or other dish. If you steam them, all the sand will settle to the bottom of the pot; you can strain the liquid before you serve it if you like.

Store soft-shell clams in the same manner as the hard-shells, being careful not to break them. They will last a day or two under refrigeration, but it's best to use them as soon as possible.

HOW TO SHUCK OYSTERS

I always thought that opening oysters was really difficult — so difficult that I never bothered to try. Being married to a fisherman who handled the job nicely, I didn't have to. Recently, I had a short lesson and found that it was not so difficult after all! Read on for instructions and a few tips from the baymen.

- A Good Oyster Knife: You need one. Go out and buy a real, honest to goodness oyster knife, used only for that purpose. The one I have is a fancy Japanese model from a store in Tribeca, with a thin, beveled, rounded blade and a wooden handle. The type that folks out here on the East End use is a Dexter/Russell model with a shorter, thicker blade and a slightly more pointed tip. The blade should be tough and not flexible; do not use a sharp knife.

- Use Protection! Use a towel or a thick glove to protect the hand that holds the oyster — something that will prevent you from slashing your hand and keep the oyster from slipping. I've advised people at the fish stand to use an oven mitt after hearing that one of my customers, an elderly French lady experienced in opening oysters, stabbed herself by accident. Don't skip this step.

- Oysters Should Be Still and Cold. You may want to put the oysters in the freezer for 15 minutes or so before you open them. This causes the muscle holding the shells together to relax somewhat and makes it a little easier to open. Avoid jostling the oysters around before opening them; that causes them to clench up and makes them tougher to open. I rinse the oysters in cold water, place them on a plate cupped side down, flat side up, and put the plate in the back of the refrigerator (or the freezer) until I am ready to open them.

1. Grip the oyster with a folded towel, glove, or an oven mitt. You want to prevent the oyster from slipping at all costs.

2. Insert the tip of the knife in the hinge of the back of the oyster. Hold the oyster with your fingers on either side of the shell and try to avoid pressing down on the oyster.

3. Wiggle the tip of the knife from side to side, then start to twist your wrist from back and forth until you feel the oyster shells give. Sometimes they will seem to pop open. Take care not to spill the oyster liquid or to scrape broken shell pieces onto the oyster.

4. Take the oyster knife and scrape the shell underneath the oyster, so no part of the oyster is stuck to the shell.

5. Carefully place the oyster onto a plate or baking sheet.

HOW TO PREPARE LOBSTER

Split a lobster before broiling or grilling it. This allows flavorings to penetrate the meat and results in an evenly cooked tail.

To Split:

1. Place the lobster on its back, hard shell down, and sever the spinal cord by inserting a sturdy knife between the tail shell and the body.

2. Starting at the head, split the lobster, cutting through the shell from head to tail.

3. Clean out the head area and discard what's inside. Remove the digestive vein that runs along the tail meat. If the lobster contains the light green tomalley, remove it (it can be saved for a sauce).

To Broil:

Split and clean a lobster. Place it on a baking sheet, shell down and meat side up, and spread it open.

Brush with oil or melted butter; add whatever spices you like (garlic, paprika, fresh herbs, etc.).

Broil about 4 inches from the flame for 10 to 12 minutes.

To Grill:

Split and clean a lobster.

Brush with oil or melted butter; add whatever spices you like (garlic, paprika, fresh herbs, etc.).

Grill shell down and meat side up for 3 to 5 minutes. Without flipping the lobster, baste it and continue to grill it meat side up for another 3 to 5 minutes.

To Steam:

Traditionally, lobsters are steamed or boiled alive and whole. If you prefer to kill the lobster first, sever its spinal cord by inserting a sturdy knife between the tail shell and the body, then immediately steam or boil it.

This method is much easier and quicker than boiling.

Put a steamer basket or an overturned plate in a large pot with a tight-fitting lid. Add about an inch or two of water and add 2 tablespoons of salt to the water. If you have seaweed, add it to the pot for extra flavor.

Heat the water until it starts to steam. Put the lobsters into the pot and cover. For 1 pounders, steam for 10 minutes; for 1 to 1 ¼ pounders, steam for 12 minutes; for 1 ¼ to 1 ½ pounders, steam for 14 minutes.

Drain, shell and serve.

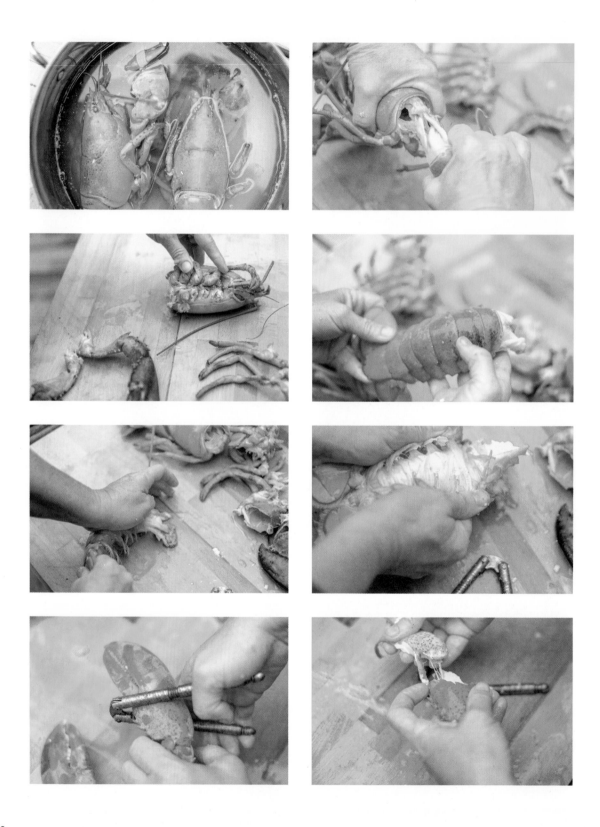

To Boil:

Set a large, salted pot of water to a boil (about 1 to 2 tablespoons salt per quart of water). If you have seaweed, add it to the pot for extra flavor.

When the water is boiling, add the lobsters to the pot headfirst and cover. Leave the rubber bands on the claws.

Boil lobsters depending on their size: for 1 pounders, boil for 8 minutes, and for 2 additional minutes per quarter pound thereafter. For a 1¼ pounder, boil for 10 minutes; for a 1½ pounder, boil for 12 minutes.

Remove from pot and let the lobsters rest for 5 minutes. They should be bright red; if they are still a brownish color, they need to cook a little longer.

When fully cooked, lobster meat should be white and firm. Any coral (roe) inside the lobster will be reddish-orange.

Cleaning After Cooking:

1. Twist off the two large claws. Crack these with a nutcracker or pliers and remove the meat. If the claws are especially hard, crack them with a hammer — enough to crack the shell but not hard enough to crush the meat. Remove any pieces of cartilage in the center of the claw meat.

2. Crack the knuckles and push the meat out from the shell. Use kitchen shears if necessary.

3. Twist the tail and remove it from the body. Twist or snap off the flippers on the bottom of the tail. Check to make sure meat is removed from the center flipper.

4. Insert your finger or a fork in the hole in the bottom of the shell and push the meat out of the shell in one piece. If necessary, pull the shell apart or use a pair of kitchen shears to cut it apart to make the meat easier to remove.

5. Pull the thin strip of meat off the back of the tail and remove the digestive vein beneath (similar to a shrimp's digestive vein).

6. Remove the green tomalley, or liver, from the head and eat as is or save for a sauce. (Many people consider the tomalley a delicacy; my family always ate it.) If there is any coral, or roe, in the head, remove it to eat as well.

Larger lobsters will have some meat in the head near where it attaches to the tail. For smaller lobsters don't bother picking out this meat.

The small legs of a lobster can be broken off and the meat sucked out as if you are sucking through a straw.

HOW TO CLEAN WHOLE SQUID

1. Start by cutting just below the eyes of the squid to free the tentacles. Remove the squid's beak (a hard, round piece of cartilage located inside the tentacles) by squeezing the tentacles and pulling it free. Discard the beak.

2. Take the squid body (or tube) in one hand and remove the entrails. They should slip away from each other quite easily. Discard the entrails.

3. Inside the squid body is a thin clear sliver of cartilage called a pen or cuttle (the squid's backbone). Remove the pen by pulling it out, then discard it. Rinse out the inside of the tube, clearing it of any digestive matter.

4. Finally, there is the squid's skin membrane. Although this dark, spotty skin is edible, most cooks choose to remove it for presentation's sake. This can be done by peeling it off with your fingers or by scraping it off with a knife.

You may leave the squid body whole or cut it into rings, depending on which recipe you are using.

HOW TO PREPARE SHRIMP

Shrimp can be shelled and cleaned before or after you cook them; it depends what you want to do with them. Generally, shrimp cooked with shells or heads on are more flavorful.

To Cook with Shells On:

Set a large, salted pot of water to a boil (about 1 to 2 tablespoons salt per quart of water). If you like, add a few tablespoons of Old Bay seasoning or any other crab/shrimp boil seasoning.

Rinse shrimp; when water is boiling add shrimp to pot. Cook for 2 to 3 minutes depending on the size of the shrimp; when shrimp float to the top of the pot they are done.

Drain and rinse with cold water.

To Clean:

1. Remove shells and reserve for stock.

2. Make a shallow cut down the back of each shrimp and remove the blackish digestive vein with the tip of a paring knife.

3. Rinse.

To Cook with Shells Off:

Set a large, salted pot of water to a boil (about 1 to 2 tablespoons per quart of water). If you like, add a few tablespoons of Old Bay seasoning or any other crab/shrimp boil seasoning.

Remove shrimp shells and reserve for stock. Make a shallow cut down the back of each shrimp and remove the blackish digestive vein with the tip of a paring knife. Rinse.

When the water is boiling, add the shrimp to pot. Cook for 2 to 3 minutes depending on the size of the shrimp; when shrimp float to the top of the pot they are done.

Remove shrimp with a slotted spoon. Strain and reserve water for stock.

HOW TO KEEP FISH
AND SHELLFISH

When you buy a piece of fish from us at the market, we recommend that you use it within two days. Fish bought on Wednesday should be used by Friday night or put in the freezer.

The notable exception is squid, which must be used within one day. Putting squid in the freezer actually makes it a little more tender, and does not really make a big difference tastewise.

Shark and skate, two fish that have cartilage instead of bones, should also be used within one day. These fish can sometimes have a strong ammonia smell if they are not exceedingly fresh. The sooner you cook them the better.

To keep fish in the refrigerator, put the bag of fish in a bowl until ready to use it. If you like you can pack the fish in ice; just make sure that the ice is not in direct contact with the fish, and that it does not sit in water.

Shellfish is best stored by taking it out of the bag and putting it in an uncovered bowl in the back of your refrigerator. Do not use ice (if the shellfish sit in water from melted ice they will die). As long as the shellfish are cold and can breathe, they will last for a few days. Generally, hard-shell clams and oysters will last 4 or 5 days; soft-shell clams and mussels will last 1 to 2 days.

If you like, you may soak the shellfish in a large pot; be sure to use salt water. A half-cup of cornmeal added to the water will cause the shellfish to spit out any sand that may be inside them.

After purging the clams, rinse under cold running water and they are ready to use.

HOW TO MAKE SHRIMP OR LOBSTER STOCK

If using lobster shells, crush them with a mallet or the back of a heavy chef's knife.

2 pounds shrimp or lobster shells

1 tablespoon canola oil

½ cup onion, diced

¼ cup carrot, diced

¼ cup celery, diced

6 to 8 cups cold water

4 or 5 stalks parsley

1 bay leaf

10 peppercorns

In a large stockpot, heat the oil over medium-low heat.

Add the onion, carrot and celery and cook until soft, about 6 to 8 minutes. Add the shrimp or lobster shells and cook for 1 minute.

Add the water and the parsley, bay leaf and peppercorns, and bring to a boil.

Turn heat down to low, partially cover the pot and simmer for 45 minutes.

Turn off the heat and let the stock cool. Strain the stock and pour into quart containers.

Stock may be frozen and defrosted as needed.

HOW TO MAKE FISH STOCK

Use any white fish racks (heads and bones) to make stock; we usually avoid the oilier fish, like bluefish or mackerel, because they impart a strong, rather gamey flavor. Remove all organs in the stomach cavity and the gills, which can leave a bitter flavor.

2 white fish racks, cleaned and gilled, stomach cavity rinsed

1 tablespoon olive oil

1 onion, peeled and chopped

1 medium carrot, peeled and chopped

2 stalks celery with leaves, chopped

10 cups cold water

4 or 5 stalks parsley

In a large stockpot, heat the olive oil over medium-low heat.

Add the onion, carrot and celery and cook until soft, about 6 to 8 minutes.

Add the fish racks and the water. Make sure the water completely covers the fish.

Add the parsley sprigs and bring to a boil. Turn heat down to low, partially cover the pot and simmer for 45 minutes.

Turn off the heat and let the stock cool. Strain the stock and pour into quart containers.

Stock may be frozen and defrosted as needed.

SMELLY BOOTS: THOUGHTS ON A DYING INDUSTRY

You know how I said squid is highly perishable? Well, in case you don't already know, what comes with expired squid is a particularly horrible smell, one likely to clear a room, if not an entire house. Fishing is sometimes a smelly business to be in, so take my word for it, nothing smells as bad as old squid.

Fishermen have been known to take advantage of this. Revenge stories abound of rancid squid being dumped on a rival's boat deck —I've even heard about a guy who broke into another's truck and poured the water that some rotting squid had been sitting in into the air conditioner vents. So much for cooling off after a hard day's work! But of all the pranks I've heard about, there's one story concerning smelly squid that beats them all.

Back in the early 80s in Hampton Bays, Long Island, the New York State Department of Environmental Conservation, or the DEC, which is charged with regulating the fishery and the fishermen, was hassling one of the fishermen who was building lobster pots in his own yard. They had issued tickets to him repeatedly, and he was getting pretty peeved. Whenever they issued a ticket, it came with a court summons, which meant a day spent on a court bench rather than on a boat or working on gear, not to mention whatever fine the judge imposed.

After receiving multiple summons, this fisherman finally had enough. That morning of his next court appearance, he got up early, took a pair of rubber boots, stabbed holes all over them and filled them up with rotten squid. When he showed up in court, he was wearing his holey boots, squishing foul squid juice all over the courtroom with every step. By the time the stench had reached the judge's bench, everyone who could had moved over to the far side of the courtroom, leaving the fisherman alone.

The judge called him up right away and, though taken aback by the smell, still managed to ask, "What are you here for?" The fisherman slapped his ticket down on the bench, then squished backward. After he read the ticket, the judge stood up and leaned over the bench to look at the man's smelly, squid-filled boots. He took one look at the fisherman's simpering grin and ordered him away for a psychiatric evaluation!

Fishermen have to go through a lot in their life's work. It's not salty stories all the time; there's a bureaucracy to deal with too. I think I can safely say that I'm speaking for all commercial fishermen when I say, the paperwork's a pain! Here are some of the requirements that commercial fishermen must meet.

Regulations

Fishermen are accountable for every pound of fish landed. They must file daily trip reports describing what kind of fish were landed, what size and how many pounds, what kind of fish were discarded and how much, the longitude and latitude where they were caught or discarded, what type and size of gear was used, the time the trip started, the time spent fishing, and the time the trip ended. This information is then double-checked with the dealer reports, which are required by whomever buys the fish from the fishermen. It's a lot to report on.

Fishing vessels can be boarded and searched by several government agencies without a warrant. Some regulations require a federal observer to be taken along on the fishing boat to monitor certain trips.

The federal government divides the fish quota among all the East Coast states. In New York State we hold licenses for different types of fish and shellfish; most fish are caught on a quarterly quota system. Some fish, like sturgeon, are closed entirely to both commercial and recreational fishing. Most regulations on how much fish one can catch during a trip change during the year. We regularly get notices in the mail saying, for example, "Black sea bass is closed until further notice." It can change from one day to the next.

Quotas and regulations are based in part on population surveys. The fish surveys done by NOAA (National Oceanic and Atmospheric Administration) are sometimes seen as inaccurate by the fishermen. For example, a recent NOAA fluke survey was done when the fluke were migrating, thus not showing their true numbers. A recent blackfish survey conducted locally counted fish at a time of year when the blackfish had moved offshore and when the local fishermen had removed their fish pots from the water because there were hardly any blackfish around to catch.

Regulatory agencies have also been known to survey fish while using fishing gear that hasn't been used in 50 years or while setting the gear improperly. In a recent positive and very welcome development, some of these agencies have begun to hire experienced fishermen to help with the surveys in order to improve the results.

Overdevelopment

Fishing requires a boat and lots of gear, so you need somewhere to put all that stuff, usually at a commercial dock. Last summer we heard that "guys in suits" were snooping around to see how many condos they could build on Mattituck Inlet —right where the commercial dock is now, along with ospreys, swans, and striped bass. Lucky for us, it didn't pan out because they couldn't build enough units to make it worth their while.

Excessive building plays a part in pushing the commercial fishermen out of traditional fishing areas. There are not too many places left for commercial boats anymore. Waterfront property is increasingly valuable, and many of the old marinas have been sold. One on Mattituck Inlet that was home to a number of commercial boats was sold to the DEC —they keep all their government boats there, as well as the Southold Police boats. Some existing marinas are run-down and in disrepair. It costs too much to restore a bulkhead and a dock and to provide water and electricity —millions of dollars— for just a few commercial boats. Marinas can make more money with the recreational boating crowd.

Besides, who wants smelly old commercial boats near their property? Fishermen leave their traps and nets and equipment by the dock. Everyone seems to think the commercial docks smell bad, but I've never seen any random loose fish lying around. All the fish that comes in is iced and packed up well, taken off the boat immediately and sold. Every so often someone comes along and dumps a couple of cats down there, as if there were piles of discarded fish for the cats to eat. There aren't. Like people who buy a house next to a farm and then complain about the smells and sounds from the farm, no one wants commercial fishermen in their backyard.

Pollution

Overdevelopment not only displaces fishermen, it also leads to pollution. When the condo developers were checking out Mattituck Inlet, I thought, "Where would their sewage go?" Right into the water, no doubt. Too much building around the Great South Bay led to septic tanks and sewage treatment plants leaching into the water, killing off all the clam beds that had produced clams in record numbers for so long.

In the Hamptons, on the North Fork and elsewhere, there are lots of big houses on the water with perfect green lawns. All the chemical fertilizers keeping those lawns looking so nice run right into the bays and creeks. That leads to an excess of nitrogen in the water, and in the summer when the water temperature warms, it often causes algal blooms: red tides and brown tides that kill off the eelgrass and the small scallops and fish in the bay.

That's what happened to Peconic Bay scallops. The bay scallop fishery, worth millions of dollars to the local economy, was decimated in 1985 by a series of brown tide algal blooms. Cornell Cooperative Extension's bay scallop restoration program, in which millions of scallops have been planted into Peconic Bay, has made some progress in bringing the bay scallop back, but they are nowhere near the numbers that we used to see.

Before the brown tide, everyone used to go fishing for bay scallops when the season opened and bring in bushel after bushel —Eastern Long Island was famous for them. Every restaurant had them (not just the fancy ones) and they were cheap, $6 per pound at the fish market. Baymen made a good living harvesting them, and locals filled up their freezers with plenty of the tiny sweet meats.

Nowadays, brown tides seem to happen every couple of years, keeping the bay scallop population smaller than anyone would like. The brown tides prevent the eelgrass from flourishing; eelgrass beds act as a nursery area for young fish, shellfish, crabs, and waterfowl. All of those populations in the Bay have suffered. This year bay scallops went for $28 per pound.

Climate Change

Fish migrate, and we catch different fish at certain times of the year. Lately this has been changing, and the fish are showing up early or late. I've stopped predicting when we will have a certain fish at the fish stand. Mackerel and herring, the cold water fish, have been coming in later and later in the year, to the point where we hardly have any herring to sell at all.

This past year sea bass showed up in May. We had gorgeous, huge sea bass that we were selling to a couple of restaurants in New York City, as well as to our regular customers. Fishermen were saying the bass should be around the Chesapeake area in May, but they were up in the Sound because the water was warmer.

Just as all was going well and there were plenty of fish, the DEC closed the sea bass fishery for the month of June, even though the state was well under the quarterly quota. It was hard to explain to customers and restaurants why we couldn't bring sea bass in to market anymore, especially since there were plenty around.

New York Senator Charles Schumer went to bat for the fishermen, who were upset that they had lost their opportunity to make some money catching one of the more valuable fish. A compromise was reached, and the fishery was reopened three weeks early in late June. Schumer called the regulations "inflexible" and "outdated."

Unfortunately, fish surveys often lag far behind what is actually happening out on the water. It seems reasonable that when fish are plentiful, we should be able to catch them to feed our families rather than buying endangered Chilean sea bass or tilapia raised in contaminated fish farms in Thailand.

Most of our local commercial fishermen are willing to abide by regulations so that our local fisheries are sustainable —no one wants to be put out of business— but fishermen don't always trust the government's data on fish stocks either, especially after seeing the regulatory agencies making mistake after mistake in surveying the fish.

United States commercial fishermen are probably the most highly regulated fishermen in the world. Extremely tough State and Federal regulations have driven many commercial fishermen to anger and despair (like the man in the story, whom we now call "smelly boots"), and have driven many out of business completely. While regulations on overfished species are necessary, other times rules and regulations based on inaccurate surveys unduly handicap the fishermen. From our experiences, we think that collaborating for better science on the water and exercising compromise seems like the best path forward for the DEC and commercial fishermen.

ACKNOWLEDGEMENTS

Thank you to everyone who helped make this book a reality. The encouragement, positivity and advice I received was amazing.

Thank you to all the commercial fishermen and women and their families near and far, especially: the Jayne Family, Jimmy and Cindy Kaminsky, Jeff and Mercy Kaminsky, the Kretchmer Family, the Migdalski Family, the Rispoli Family, and the Szczotka Family. It's not an easy way to make a living but we make it work. I appreciate all the help you've given us in so many ways. Thank you to Jimmy Coronesi, Diane David, Greg Morgese and Mario Robles for your support —we couldn't do it without you.

For publishing and marketing advice, thanks to Stephanie Abarbanel, Chris Benton, Lisa Cosby, Adeline Driscoll, Anna Dunn, Susanna Einstein, Roy Finamore, Peter Frandsen, Carolyn Graham, Paul Greenberg, Ria Julien, Tommy Marino, Deb Piaseczynski, and Regina Schrambling.

Thanks to all the chefs who generously contributed recipes and who support us at the Greenmarket: Ray Bradley, Rocco DiSpirito, Marc Forgione, Robin Puskas, Carmen Quagliata, Alex Raij, Phet Schwader, Hiroko Shimbo, Ed Sun, David Tanis, and Simpson Wong.

Thanks to all the folks who kindly shared their recipes: Jake Henry, Gerard Mossé, Larry Racies, Erika Sipos, Harry Smith, Laing Laing Wan, and Ruggero Vanni.

Thank you GrowNYC and Greenmarket staff, and all the farmers and producers in the market. What a wonderful community we have created. It's a pleasure to work with you, tough out the weather with you, and joke around with you each week.

To the fishmongers, we couldn't have done it without you. To all of our customers both old and new, you are the reason we keep doing what we do! Thank you from the bottom of my heart for your support.

To Alex and Ruby, thanks for being patient through all the questions, fish cooking experiments, photo shoots and general craziness. Alex, I appreciate your many, many hours of hard work. Ruby, thanks for being a great stylist!

To all of our family and friends, I have appreciated your longtime support and encouragement. Thank you!

To Sally Mara Sturman and Jean Andrews, thank you for your help with styling, recipe testing and proofreading.

To Elvira Morán, thank you for your wonderful design skills, your enthusiasm and your desire to see this project come to life.

To Kevin Bay, thank you for keeping fish on the brain for so long! I appreciate all the time and hard work you put into this project including editing, photography, and general fish wrangling. So glad we were able to laugh all the way through this experience.

— Stephanie Villani

For love and support, advice, equipment, mentorship, inspiration and recipe testing, thanks to the following: Michael Azerrad, Kathy Bay, Kevin and Jackie Bay, Anna Dunn, Susanna Einstein, Beth Gill, Peter Glebo, María Fernanda González Olivo, Topher Gross, John Hicks, Aaron Hodges, Michael and Susan Kleinberg, Luke Kummer, Eliane Liu, MaryAnn and Bruce Lucas, Sara Lucas, Ed Menashy, Justin Peake, Jack Porobil, Yannic and Theresa Rack, Ben Rauch and Margaret Scott, Andrew Samuel, Ryan Seaton, Daniela Serna, Mauricio Serna, Rush and Stacy Simpson, Lauren Smith, Thomas Stephanos, Sally Mara Sturman, Tommy Tune, Alex Villani, Ruby Villani, and Robert Witherow.

To Elvira Morán: this would not have been possible without your help from the very beginning. Thank you for your many, many hours making our book beautiful!

And to Stephanie Villani: I'll never forget this incredible experience, all the hard work writing and testing recipes with our primary taste-tester Alex Villani, and weekend photoshoots with the inimitable nine-year old stylist Ruby Villani. Thank you for everything!

—Kevin Bay

INDEX

ABOUT THE AUTHORS

Stephanie Villani and her fisherman husband run Blue Moon Fish from the North Fork of Long Island. They have been selling local fish, shellfish and smoked fish at NYC Greenmarkets since 1988. She is a member of the Farmer and Community Advisory Committee with the GrowNYC Greenmarket program and blogs at www.bluemoonfish.com.

Kevin Bay is a photographer, writer and former fishmonger living in New York City. More about his work can be found at www.searobinstudios.com.

Elvira Morán is a graphic designer and fishmonger. Originally from northern Spain she has lived in New York City since 1992. Designing this book has been the best of her two worlds coming together. You can see her work at www.elviradesigns.com

Published in the United States by
Breakwater Media

www.bluemoonfish.com

Library of Congress Cataloging-in-Publication
data is on file with the publisher.

Hardcover ISBN: 978-1-5323-2384-3

Printed in China

Designed by Elvira Morán

First Edition